ETHNIC CHRONOLOGY SERIES
NUMBER 24

The Russians in America
A Chronology & Fact Book

Compiled and edited by

Vladimir Wertsman

1977
OCEANA PUBLICATIONS, INC.
DOBBS FERRY, NEW YORK

Library of Congress Cataloging in Publication Data

Wertsman, Vladimir, 1929-
   The Russians in America, 1727-1975.

   (Ethnic chronology series ; no. 24)
   Bibliography: p.
   Includes index.
   SUMMARY: A history of Russians in America in chronology
format, with a selection of illustrative documents, appendices,
and bibliography.
   1. Russian Americans—History—Chronology. 2. Russian Americans—
History—Sources. [1. Russian Americans—History] I. Title. II. Series.
E184.R9W47   973'.04'9171   76-7416
ISBN 0-379-00522-0

Manufactured in the United States of America

TABLE OF CONTENTS

EDITOR'S FOREWORD

Russian Americans comprise a relatively small ethnic community of about 750,000 people spread all over the United States. Heavier concentrations of Russian Americans can be found in the states of California, New Jersey, New York, and Pennsylvania. They are predominantly of Russian Orthodox faith, but there are also Catholic and Protestant groups. Russian Americans are hard workers, modest and very ingenious. Although they represent a tiny segment of the total United States population, Russian Americans made substantial and various contributions to our country, especially in the fields of agriculture, engineering, music, ballet, writing and higher education; Vladimir Zworykin in electronics and Igor Sikorsky in aeronautics, Serge Rachmaninoff and Igor Stravinsky in music, Igor Youskevitch and George Balanchine in ballet, Vladimir Nabokov in literature, Pitirim Sorokin in sociology and Wassily Leontief in economics, are just a few examples from a list of numerous prominent Russian American personalities who are going to be encountered in this book.

This book was designed to provide basic information on Russian Americans. It contains a chronological section of important events in the life of Russian Americans, a selection of relevant documents, an annotated bibliography guiding to further research, an appendix of Russian American organizations and institutions, influential periodicals, American colleges and universities offering courses in Russian, and statistical tables. Although intended primarily as an introduction to reference materials for secondary school and community college students, the book should prove a valuable aid to teachers, scholars, historians, and others interested in ethnic studies.

In the preparation of this volume, I have been assisted by numerous institutions and individuals. Acknowledgement goes first to the Brooklyn Public Library, Columbia University Library, Harvard Russian Research Center, Hoover Institution, New York Public Library, San Francisco Public Library, Sitka Historical Society, Tolstoy Foundation, and the University of Pittsburgh Library; also to the National Geographic and Travel magazines for permission to reprint materials included in the documents section. Secondly, I would like to express my sincere thanks to my good friends, Palmar Brynildsen, Arline Cohen, Martin Dooley, Alice Hauser, Henri Veit, Barbara Ann Watters, Walter Wolff, and Paul Zaplitny for their devoted cooperation.

Vladimir Wertsman
Brooklyn Public Library
Brooklyn, New York

1727   August 16. The first Russian presence in America was
                recorded. A Russian Navy expedition, conducted by
                Captain Vitus Bering, reached Saint Lawrence Island,
                now part of Alaska. The expedition was designed to
                map Siberian Arctic regions and to verify that Siberia
                is connected with America by land.

1741   July 15-16. The first Russians landed on Alaskan soil.
                A new Russian expedition led by Captain Vitus Bering
                and Shipmaster Aleksei Chirikov sighted Mount Saint
                Elias in Southern Alaska and landed on Kayak Island.

                December 8. On his way back to Russia, Captain Vitus
                Bering died of scurvy. He was buried on the island
                bearing his name. Two other places - Bering Strait
                and Bering Sea - were also named after the daring cap-
                tain.

1740s-1750s   After returning to Russia, the surviving members of
                Bering's expedition found out with amazement that the
                furs of the sea animals they hunted were worth about
                30,000 dollars. Lured by the prospect of fabulous
                profits, Russian fur hunters, fur traders, adventurers,
                etc. - called promyshlenniki - swept the Alaskan coast
                and its islands. The local inhabitants - Aleuts,
                Tlingits, Eskimos - were reduced to slavery or forced
                to pay tribute, while the animal resources were savage-
                ly exploited.

1762   The rebellion of the Aleuts took place. After long
                suffering on the hands of Russian explorers, the Aleuts
                formed a secret confederation from the Peninsula of
                Alaska to the Umak Islands, then caught and destroyed
                four Russian ships landed on the Fox Islands, and mas-
                sacred the greatest part of the crews. A fifth ship,
                headed by Stepan Glotov, which passed the Fox Islands
                and the Alaska Peninsula, discovered and explored Ko-
                diak Island.

1770s-1780s   New Russian expeditions explored Unalaska, Kayak Island,
                and a part of the Alaskan mainland. During one of these
                expeditions, Potap Zaikov discovered the Copper River,
                and entered Prince William Sound. The Russians named
                it Chugach, a name retained to this day for the moun-
                tains bordering the north shore of the sound.

1784   August. The first Russian settlement in Alaska was
                founded on Kodiak Island by Grigori Shelikhov and named
                Three Saints Bay. The new settlement had 192 people,
                and the only woman among them was Natalia Shelikhov,
                wife of Grigori and the first Russian woman to set
                foot on American soil. Grigori Shelikhov was the co-

owner of the Shelikhov-Golikov Company, a wealthy
fur trading company.

1785   Grigori Shelikhov established the first Russian school
at Three Saints Bay, and personally instructed the
pupils in Russian, arithmetic, and basic Christianity.

1790   The first marriage between a Russian and a native woman of Kodiak Island took place. The ceremony of marriage was performed by a Russian Navy priest belonging
to the crew of the ship Glory of Russia landed at Three
Saints Bay. Several mixed marriages followed in the
ensuing years, and the children born from such marriages were called "creoles," but they had the same
rights as Russian children.

1791   July 27. Alexander Baranov, the new manager of the
Shelikhov-Golikov Company, arrived at the Three Saints
Bay and became the chief figure of the Russian settle-
ment for almost three decades.

1792   Prince Dimitrius Galitzin, son of a Russian ambassador
in Europe, who came to the United States on a visit,
converted to Catholicism, became a priest and settled
in America. He spent the rest of his life among Indians
and frontier farmers and displayed legendary facts of
bravery, charity and tolerance.

The Holy Synod of the Russian Orthodox Church sent out
a special mission of monks to minister to the colonists
and their converts, and the first Orthodox church, St.
Nicholas, was built in America.

1793   Alexander Baranov established a well equipped brass
and iron foundry near present Sitka, Alaska, where
very heavy bells were cast and sold to the Franciscan
missions of California.

1794   August. The Russians built their first ship in Alaska
on the southern side of Kensai Peninsula. The ship
was called Resurrection and had a burden of 180 tons.
It was seventy-three feet long, twenty-three feet wide,
and thirteen feet deep.

1796   A new Russian colony was established at Yakutat. It
was called New Russia, and it consisted of only two
buildings (one for hunters, and the second for colonists
and their families), but it facilitated the Russian advancement about 400 miles to the east along the Alaskan mainland.

1799   July. Alexander Baranov established a trading post

at Fort St. Michael, a few miles north of the present
Sitka. This settlement helped the Russians in advancing about 200 miles to the south.

December 27. The Russian American Company obtained
its first fur trade charter, and secured monopolistic
rights to the fur trade of all Russian possessions in
America. The Russian American Company came into existence by the merger of the former Shelikhov-Golikov
Company with another competitive company. Its main
organizer was Nicholas Rezanov.

1802
June 20. Tlingit tribes, whom the Russians called
Kolosh, attacked and destroyed the Russian colony at
Fort St. Michael. They also attacked a group of Rus-
sians at Sea Otter Bay and massacred about 200 people.
Only forty-two women and children survived.

1804
September 29 to October 6. Alexander Baranov and two
Russian vessels under the command of Captain Yuri
Lisiansky recaptured the Russian colony after a battle
that lasted a week. The Tlingits lost thirty men.
Baranov reestablished the Russian colony and named it
New Archangel, while the fort of the colony was called
Redoubt Archangel Michael. Both were on the site of
Sitka, Alaska. Sitka became the main Pacific port of
North America and also the capital of Russian America.

1805
Nicholas Rezanov, the main leader of the Russian American Company and chamberlain of the Russian emperor, inspected the Russian settlements in America and established a school and a library in Sitka.

1806
Nicholas Rezanov attempted to enter the Columbia River,
but was not able to cross the bar. He later entered
the Golden Gate, anchored in San Francisco, and established friendly relations with the Spaniards at Yerba
Buena.

1807-1808
Several new Russian ships, Avos, Sitka, Otkritie, etc.,
were built at Sitka in order to stimulate the colonial
commerce. One of the vessels was constructed under
the supervision of an American called Lincoln, and the
shipyard was in front of the present post-office building of Sitka.

1812
September 12. The first Russian settlement was established in California. The settlement was named Fort
Ross and was located eight miles above the Russian
River in Sonoma County. Fort Ross was settled by
ninety-five Russians and eighty Aleuts who were sent
from Sitka by Baranov in order to produce agricultural

products for Alaska. The leader of the Fort Ross settlers was Ivan Kuskov.

1818 April 16. After being relieved of his function as
general manager of the Russian American Company,
Alexander Baranov died on his way back to Russia. He
was burried at sea opposite Princes Island in the water
of the Indian Ocean. His memory was immortalized by
such places as Baranov Castle, Baranov Hill, Baranov
Island, and others.

1821 The Russian American Company got its second fur trading charter, preserving all monopolistic rights over
the Russian possessions in America for twenty years.
(See 1799)

1824 April 5 to 17. The United States, England, and Russia
signed a treaty for a ten year period, limiting the
boundary of Russian possessions in America at 54°40'
northern latitude.

July 29. The Russian priest Ivan Veniaminov came to
Alaska as a missionary. He learned the Aleutian language, translated main parts of the Bible from Russian
into Aleutian, and using his oratoric gift, became
very successful in converting the natives to Christianity. "When he preached the word of God, all people
listened, and listened without moving....," recalled
a native. At the time of Veniaminov's arrival, many
Russian Orthodox churches were already in existence in
Alaska.

1834 Lieutenant N. Zarembo of the Russian Navy established
Redoubt St. Dionysus on the site of the present town
of Wrangell, near the north end of Wrangell Island,
Alaska. The action was taken by the Russians to prevent an English settlement.

1837 The Baranov Castle was built in Sitka to replace the
original building erected by Baranov as the residence
of the chief managers of the Russian American Company.
The site is now occupied by the United States Department of Agriculture.

1840 Father Ivan Veniaminov became the first Russian Orthodox bishop of Alaska. It was a reward for his excep-
tional missionary work among the Aleuts and Tlingits.
Veniaminov also made important scientific contributions
by publishing a three volume compendium called Notes
of the Islands of the Unalaska District. This work
remains to our days a basic text on the ethnology and
other features of the region.

Captain Adolph Etolin became the general manager of
the Russian American Company. Using his experience
as a former assistant manager of the same company,
Etolin established friendly relations with the natives
and made them very cooperative.

Father Dimitrius Galitzin died and was buried in his
churchyard at Loretto, Pennsylvania. Galitzin was the
first Catholic priest to receive all his orders and
training in the United States. (See 1792)

1841   A church school was opened at Sitka. Later it was
raised to the rank of seminary. It had a good library
equipped with Russian and Slavonic books.

The centennial of Bering's voyages and discoveries was
marked in New Archangel by the launching of the first
steam vessel in the Pacific. The vessel was named
Nicholas I, after the Russian emperor, and it was entirely built on the New Archangel shipyard, except for
a sixty-horsepower engine, which came from the United
States.

The Russians sold Fort Ross in California to Captain
John Sutter, a Swiss, for the sum of 30,000 dollars
and the Russian settlers returned to Sitka, Alaska.
(See 1812)

1844   October 10. The Russian American Company obtained its
third charter and maintained all former privileges.
In addition, it had given to the children of Russian
fathers and native women the same rights as to all
Russian tradesmen. (See 1821)

The Russian Orthodox Cathedral of St. Michael was
built in Sitka.

1845   Captain Michael Tebenkov collected the charts of Alaskan waters, made new surveys and published an atlas
entitled The Northwest Coast of America from Bering
Strait to Cape Corrientos and the Aleutian Islands.
Tebenkov was assisted by two natives, and the first
edition of the atlas was published in Sitka, Alaska.

1855   A revolt of the Tlingits against the Russians marked
the last outburst of natives against Russian rule.
(See 1802)

1857   The Countinghouse of the Russian American Company (for
the counting of furs), later used by the United States
as the Governor's Office, and the Customhouse were
built in Sitka, Alaska.

1858   The General Colonial Institute was opened in Sitka for
            the sons of the officials who rendered faithful service
            to the Russian American Company. Navigation, commer-
            cial branches, and English were taught by naval of-
            ficers. Later, the General College for Russians was
            opened. Its curriculum included modern languages,
            mathematics, various branches of science, navigation,
            etc.

1861   According to the census, the Russian settlements in
            Alaska were inhabited by 576 Russian men and 208 Rus-
            sian women. At the same time, Alaska had forty-three
            communities with thirty-five chapels and nine Russian
            Orthodox churches attended by about 12,000 native
            Christians, of whom many were of mixed blood and had
            Russian names. Church services were conducted in both
            Russian and Aleutian languages.

            John Basil Turchin (born Ivan Vasilevich Turchinov),
            who came to the United States in 1856, was appointed
            colonel of the 19th Illinois Volunteers Regiment. He
            served with his regiment in Missouri, Kentucky, and
            Alabama, and took part in the capture of Huntsville
            and Decatur. For his courage, exceptional military
            actions and ingenious contributions, Turchin was pro-
            moted to the rank of U.S. brigadier general. He was
            the first and only Russian-American general who fought
            for the Union's cause.

1861-1863   Russian trading expeditions reached Nuklukayet, Alaska
            at the mouth of the Tanana. The interests of the Rus-
            sian American Company often conflicted with the expand-
            ing interests of the Hudson's Bay Company, since these
            companies were bitter competitors for the trade along
            the rivers flowing into the Pacific and the Arctic.
            These conditions combined with the increasing conflicts
            between the Russians and the natives, as well as the
            depletion of the fur resources in Alaska, precipitated
            the Alaskan deal between Russia and the United States.

1867   March 30. William H. Seward, secretary of state of
            the United States, concluded a treaty with Russia,
            under which Russia sold all its American possessions -
            the Alaskan mainland and islands - to the United States
            for the sum of 7,200,000 dollars. The treaty provided
            also that the Alaskan inhabitants will enjoy "all
            rights, privileges, and immunities of citizens of the
            United States."

            October 18. The transfer of Alaska from Russian ad-
            ministration to American administration was celebrated.
            To the beat of drums, a Russian military unit under

the command of Captain Aleksei Peschurov, and an American military unit led by Generals Lovell Rousseau and
Jeff Davis, were brought to attention and as one flag
came down and the other went up, salutes were alter-
nately given by Russian and American guns.

December 31. The last manager of the Russian American
Company, Dimitri Maksutov, his family, and 300 Russians
left Sitka and returned to Russia. Other Russians left
for Canada, while a part of them moved to San Francisco,
California. Some Russians, however, together with
thousands of descendents from mixed marriages (Russians
and native women) remained under American administration in Alaska.

1868   March 1. The Reverend Agapius Honcharenko, a newly
        arrived immigrant, began publishing the Alaskan Herald
        in San Francisco, California. The new publication, a
        biweekly newspaper published in English and Russian,
        was addressed to the Russian speaking population of
        Alaska and California and helped bridge the cultural
        gap between the above population and the rest of the
        English speaking citizens of the United States.

1870   The first Russian Orthodox parish was organized in
        New York City at 941 Second Avenue. Services were
        held in both Slavonic and English languages. The
        parish periodical called Oriental Church Magazine was
        published in English only.

1872   The headquarters of the Russian Orthodox bishop was
        moved from Sitka, Alaska, to San Francisco, California.

        The official name of the Russian Orthodox Church in
        our country at that time was the Russian Orthodox
        Greek Catholic Church of America.

1880s   Russian mass immigration to the United States began.
        Compared to other ethnic groups who came from Russia
        at this time (Jews, Germans, Mennonites, Ukrainians),
        the Russian stock was numerically smaller. Several
        settlements were named after Russian cities, such as
        Moscow (Idaho), Odessa (West Texas), Odessa (Washing-
        ton), and others.

1881   The Russian Orthodox Cathedral was inaugurated in San
        Francisco, California, at 1715 Powell Street by Bishop
        Nestor.

1884   The Russian Orthodox Church of America reestablished
        two schools in Alaska, and in a few years the number
        of schools grew to seventeen.

1888   The Russian businessman, Peter Damianov, later known
                as Peter Demens, founded the city of St. Petersburg,
                Florida. It was named after the capital of Imperial
                Russia and was the birth place of Damianov.

1891   Carnegie Hall of New York City was completed by a
                group of designers, among whom Vladimir Stolyshnikov
                played an important role.

1895   The Russian Orthodox Society of Mutual Aid was founded.
                Its aim was to spread and strengthen the Russian Ortho-
                dox faith in America and to provide insurance for its
                members.

                April 25. The Holy Ghost Russian Orthodox church
                was built in Bridgeport, Connecticut. It was the
                first Russian Orthodox church in New England, and
                the seventh in the United States.

1898   A Russian Orthodox missionary school was opened in
                Minneapolis, Minnesota, to prepare new priests. Great
                stress was put on the study of English and on the trans-
                lation of Orthodox church services from Russian into
                English.

1900   The Russian Brotherhood Society was founded as a re-
                sult of a split in the Ukrainian People's Society.
                It served as a mutual aid society, rival to the Rus-
                sian Orthodox Society of Mutual Aid. (See 1895)

1900s-1910s   Continuation of Russian mass immigration to the United
                States. The immigrants were driven from their native
                country by precarious economic conditions, but especial-
                ly by religious and political persecutions. The wave
                lasted about two decades, and the newly arrived immi-
                grants settled in or around New York City, Detroit,
                Chicago, Pittsburgh, Philadelphia, Jersey City, Cleve-
                land, San Francisco, etc. The mass of Russians
                brought with them a will and capacity to work hard,
                and took the first positions that were available in
                urban communities.

1901   Brigadier General John B. Turchinov died at the age
                of seventy-nine. A few years before his death, he
                published a book entitled The Campaign and Battle of
                Chickamaugo and made several contributions to military
                journals. (See 1861)

                May 22. The St. Nicholas Russian Orthodox Cathedral
                was founded at 15 East 97 Street in New York City.

1904   Russko-Amerikansky Pravoslavny Vestnik (Russian-

American Orthodox Messenger) was published as a monthly featuring religious news and guidance for the Russian Orthodox clergy and laity. It still appears today.

1905   Nauka (Science), the largest Russian cultural-educational society, was organized in New York City. Societies of the same type were soon organized in Boston, Massachusetts, and other cities.

The Russian Orthodox Theological Seminary of North America was founded in Minneapolis, Minnesota, replacing the former Russian Orthodox Missionary School.

The headquarters of the Russian Orthodox bishop were moved from San Francisco, California, to New York City.

1905-1907   About 5,000 Russians belonging to the Molokan religious sect left Russia, and established themselves in Los Angeles, California. They were forced to leave Russia because of religious persecutions. The Molokans broke away from the Russian Orthodox Church in the eighteenth century and refused to keep the fast during Lent. They also refused to serve in the army.

1906   The Russian Symphonic Orchestra was established in New York City. It was sponsored by a group of philanthropists headed by Mrs. Margaret Wilson, daughter of President Woodrow Wilson.

St. Tikhon's Monastery, the first Russian Orthodox monastery in America, was founded in South Cannan, Pennsylvania.

The San Francisco earthquake destroyed the Russian Orthodox cathedral. A new cathedral was built at 1520 Greene Street in San Francisco, California, where it stands today.

1907   The Russian Orthodox Catholic Women's Mutual Aid Society was founded in Pittsburgh, Pennsylvania. It was created as an insurance society and for philanthropic activities.

1910   Novoye Russkoe Slovo (New Russian Word), the oldest Russian American newspaper in existence, was founded in New York City. It still has a circulation of about 30,000 and provides coverage on national and international news, as well as other subjects.

The St. Nicholas Russian Orthodox Cathedral of New York

City organized a remarkable choir conducted by Rev.
Alexander Horovetzky. The choir became well known
all over the United States and was later invited to
the White House by President Woodrow Wilson. The
main sponsor of the choir was Charles R. Crane, an
American millionaire and a great lover of Russian
church music.

1912   The Russian Orthodox Fraternity Liubov was founded in
        Jermyn, Pennsylvania, as a fraternal life insurance
        company.

        The Russian Orthodox Theological Seminary was moved
        from Minneapolis, Minnesota, to Tenafly, New Jersey.

1914   Before the beginning of World War I it was estimated
        that about 50,000 Russian immigrants settled in the
        United States. They had 169 Russian Orthodox churches
        with several dozens of priests, Saturday schools for
        children with instruction in Bible, Russian language
        and history, etc.

        The Russian Orthodox All Saints church was organized
        in Detroit, Michigan.

1915   The United Russian Orthodox Brotherhood of America
        was created in Pittsburgh, Pennsylvania, as a frater-
        nal life insurance organization.

1917   Russky Golos (The Russian Voice) started appearing as
        a weekly in New York City. It is still in existence
        and furnishes general, national, and international,
        as well as local news.

        A school for technical education was established in
        New York City by a group of educated Russian immi-
        grants under the leadership of engineer M. Koshkin.

1918   The second wave of Russian mass immigration to the
        United States began. It was caused by the October
        1917 Bolshevic Revolution and the transformation of
        Russia into a Communist dictatorship. Thousands of
        immigrants, mostly members of the upper and middle
        classes, army officers and professionals, left Russia
        to save their lives, and settled in or around the old-
        er centers of Russian settlements. (See 1890s-1900s)

        The Russian Collegiate Institute was established in
        New York City under the leadership of Professor A.
        Petrunkevich. A similar school was founded in Chi-
        cago, Illinois, and headed by Professor I. K. Nova-
        kovsky.

The Fund for the Relief of Russian Writers and Scientists was founded in New York City as an organization for sponsoring lectures and concerts, and conducting appeals for donations to aid Russian intellectuals who were forced to go into exile by the Communist regime.

Some Russian Americans assembled in such organizations as The Union of Russian Workers, Society for the Help of Russia, etc., expressed their admiration for the 1917 Bolshevic Revolution, and helped in the formation of The American Communist Party. They were opposed, however, by the majority of Russian Americans who had different views.

Sergei Rachmaninoff, world-famous composer, concert pianist and conductor, settled in the United States. He toured the country extensively and continued his creative activities during the following two decades with great success. Rachmaninoff made his American debut in 1909.

November 20. Serge Prokofiev, another world-famous composer and conductor who left Russia after the Bolshevic Revolution, made his American debut in New York City, giving a piano recital featuring his own works. Prokofiev later returned to Russia.

December 11. Nicholas Sokoloff conducted the first concert of the Cleveland Orchestra. Under Sokoloff's leadership the orchestra expanded its programs and grew to national significance in the following decades. Sokoloff came to the United States in 1903.

1919   Clergy and laymen of the Russian Orthodox church held a convention in Pittsburgh, Pennsylvania, and expressed their desire to be an autonomous body, free from pressure by religious representatives dispatched and directed by Soviet authorities.

1920   Russkaia Zhizn (Russian Life) a publication dedicated to the services of the Russian American community, was started in San Francisco, California, and is still in existence. It embraces a conservative American point of view.

Russian American church groups and priests who were opposed to the Communist regime in Russia formed the Russian Orthodox Church Outside Russia, and severed all ties with the patriarch of Moscow.

United States legal authorities arrested scores of Russian Americans belonging to the American Communist

Party, and suppressed the radical papers <u>Pravda</u> (The Truth), <u>Novyi</u> <u>Mir</u> (New World) for advocating the overthrowing of the United States Government by force.

1921 The Russian Student Fund was established in New York City as an organization helping non-Communist students of Russian birth who intended to become American citizens and complete their education in American colleges or universities.

October 29 to November 12. At the America's Making Exhibit held in New York City, the Russian Section was very active (musical festivals, art exhibits, etc.) and attracted a lot of visitors.

Feodor Chaliapin, one of the world's great opera singers, joined the Metropolitan Opera of New York City, achieving great acclaim for his interpretation of Boris Godunov in the opera with the same name by Modest Mussorgsky.

1923 Igor Sikorsky, noted aeronautical engineer, formed the Sikorsky Aero Engineering Corporation, which produced the 14-passenger S-29 plane, one of the first twin-engine planes made in America. A few years later, he organized the Sikorsky Manufacturing Corporation, which built the S-38 flying boats and several other flying models.

The Association of Russian Imperial Naval Officers in America was created in New York City as a mutual aid organization. It also organized a library and collected documents related to the history of the Russian Imperial Navy.

The Russian Orthodox Theological Seminary was transferred from Tenafly, New Jersey, to New York City, but soon was closed due to financial difficulties.

Many Russian immigrants who came to the United States via Constantinople, Turkey, organized a parish and established the Church of Christ the Saviour at 51 East 121 Street in New York City. They founded the Russian Orthodox Church in Exile, independent from the Russian Orthodox Greek Catholic Church of America.

1924 March 20 to April 4. The Russian Orthodox Church of America held a convention in Detroit, Michigan, and proclaimed herself a self-governing body. The convention condemned the repressions organized by the Soviet authorities against several leaders of the Orthodox Church in Russia.

1925   Michael Rostovtzev, noted archaelogist and historian,
        who came from Russia at the beginning of 1920, joined
        Yale University, where he taught for the next twenty
        years with distinction and became an author of several
        scholarly books.

        Igor Stravinsky, one of the greatest musicians of our
        time, made his first visit to the United States. He
        directed many important American symphonic orchestras
        and included his own compositions, such as Petrouchka
        and Rite of Spring.

        Michael Fokine, famous dancer and choreographer, came
        to the United States and started his own company in
        New York City. He previously achieved fame in Europe
        with his outstanding Ballet Russe (Russian Ballet)
        which had an influence upon the development of the
        American ballet.

        Dimitri Tiomkin, composer and musical director, settled
        in Los Angeles, California, and became one of the most
        prolific composers for Hollywood films during the next
        several decades.

        The Russian Consolidated Mutual Aid Society and the
        American Russian Slavonic Democratic Club were founded
        in New York City. The second organization served as
        an affiliate of the Democratic National Committee.

1926   The Society of Russian Veterans of World War I of San
        Francisco, California, started publishing Vestnik
        Obschestva Russkih Veteranov Velikoi Voiny (Messenger
        of the Russian Veterans of World War I) to save memoirs
        of former Russian military men.

        The Russian Children's Welfare Society was founded in
        New York City to help sick and orphaned Russian child-
        ren, victims of the Communist regime in Russia. The
        society is still in existence and it provides medical
        care and scholarships.

1927   Professor George Vernadsky, an authority on early Rus-
        sian history, settled in the United States and joined
        the Faculty of Yale University, where he taught for
        the next three decades. He published several scholar-
        ly books.

        The Federated Russian Orthodox Clubs was founded. It
        unites several clubs for young women and men of Russian
        Orthodox faith, organized for religious, cultural,
        charitable, social, and athletic purposes.

1928   The Holy Trinity Monastery of Jordanville, New York

published the semi-monthly _Pravoslavnaia_ _Russ_ (Orthodox Russia) devoted to religious aspects of life of
the Russian Orthodox Church outside Russia.

The _Novaya_ _Zarya_ (New Dawn) started publication as an
independent Russian daily in San Francisco, California.

1929   Vladimir Zworykin, an electronics engineer who came to
the United States after the Bolshevic takeover in Russia, became a research scientist for the Radio Corporation of America (RCA) and made several inventions in
the field of television.

Gregor Piatigorsky, cellist, came to the United States
and became professor of music at the University of
California, where he taught for several years.

February 19. A Russian battery of war veterans was
officially enroled as a unit of the New York National
Guard under the name of Second Combat Train of the
244th Coast Artillery.

1930   Pitirim Sorokin, a noted sociologist, established and
headed at Harvard University a new department of sociology, which became one of the major centers of
social sciences in the United States. Sorokin published several articles and scholarly books.

The Patriarchal Russian Orthodox Vicariate in America
started issuing a bi-monthly entitled _One_ _Church_,
featuring religious news and guidance for followers
of the Orthodox faith.

1931   Wassily Leontief, reputed economist, joined the Harvard
University faculty and later held several economic ad-
visory positions for the United States Government and
different organizations at home and abroad. Leontief
later originated and developed the widely acclaimed
input-output analysis used in economic planning and
in forecasting output and growth requirements.

Michael Florinsky, noted economist and teacher, took
his P.H.D. at Yale and joined the faculty of Columbia
University, where he became professor emeritus for his
outstanding teaching and scholarly activities. He is
the author of several books and contributor to specialty journals.

The Russian Independent Mutual Aid Society was founded
in Chicago, Illinois, with about 1,500 members.

Igor Sikorsky built the S-40, the first large American
four-engine plane. A few years later he built the

S-42, pioneering trans-Pacific and trans-Atlantic commercial flights. (See 1923)

Boris Bakhmetieff, professor of mechanics and hydraulics,
joined the faculty of Columbia University, New York,
where he taught for the next two decades and became
professor emeritus.

1933   George Balanchine, famous choreographer and dominant
figure in American ballet till our day, came to the
United States and opened the School of American Ballet.

Nicholas Nabokov the composer settled in the United
States and taught music at Peabody Conservatory of
Music in Baltimore, Maryland, for the next two decades.
He became the author of several compositions and wrote
for several musical journals in the United States and
Europe.

Gregory Tschebotarioff joined the faculty of Princeton
University, New Jersey, where he taught civil engineering for the next two decades. He is the author of more
than eighty articles and several books on soil and
foundation engineering.

Rossia (Russia), a semi-weekly publication, started
appearing in New York City. It is still in existence
and covers general news.

1934   Alexander Kerensky of New York, lawyer and former head
of the Russian Provisional Government after the February 1917 Revolution, published a book entitled The
Crucification of Liberty. It appeared at a time when
the terror, purging campaign, and trials intensified
in Soviet Russia, taking the lives of millions of innocent people.

The Synod of Bishops of the Russian Orthodox Church
started publishing Tserkovnaya Zhizn (Church Life),
an irregular publication regarding church events and
ecclesiastical issues.

The Association of Russian Imperial Officers started
publishing Bulletin to maintain contact among former
Russian Imperial Navy Officers. (See 1923)

November 21. The Russian Orthodox Church of America
held a convention in Cleveland, Ohio, and elected
Bishop Theophilus Pashkovsky of San Francisco, California, as its metropolitan.

1935   Boris Sergievsky, a famous test pilot and holder of

several aeronautical records in the United States, was
awarded the medal "For Excellence in Aviation" by the
American Legion.

Wladimir Woytinsky and Emma Woytinsky, husband and wife,
came to the United States, settled in Washington, D.C.,
and distinguished themselves as prominent economists,
writers and workers for different United States agen-
cies.

1936   January 2. Vladimir Zworykin and Dr. Arthur Morton
invented the electronic tube, and described their invention at a meeting of the American Association for
the Advancement in Science held in St. Louis, Montana.
The electronic tube enabled man to see in the dark.
(See 1929)

B. Bakhmeteff, a former Soviet ambassador who became
a successful American industrialist, created a $1,400,000
fund at Columbia University, New York, to expand its Russian studies program. The fund was part of a foundation
to foster advancement of Russian culture in the United
States.

1938   Igor Youskevitch, ballet dancer, made his American
debut, settled in the United States, and at the beginning of World War II joined the United States Navy,
where he served until the conclusion of the war.

The Russian Orthodox Church of America celebrated the
950th Jubilee of the baptizing of the Russian people
by Prince Vladimir, later declared a saint. At the
same time, the Russian Orthodox Seminary was reopened
in New York City and received the name of St. Vladimir's
Theological Seminary, which is still in existence.

The Russian Nobility Association in America was founded
in New York City. Its purpose was to compile records
of immigration of former Russian nobles to America and
to provide assistance to needy members.

July 8. The Russian Classroom was officially opened
at the University of Pittsburgh in Pennsylvania, featuring furniture, embroidery, and ornamental hardware
in the Russian Byzantine tradition. It was designed
by Dr. Andrew Avinoff, director of the Carnegie Museum
in Pittsburgh at that time.

December 20. Vladimir Zworykin invented the electronic
television system using the iconoscope. The patent of
invention was assigned to the Westinghouse Electric
and Manufacturing Company of Pittsburgh, Pennsylvania.
(See 1936)

1939   The 30th Anniversary of Sergei Rachmaninoff's appearance in the United States was celebrated. In a cycle
of three concerts held in Philadelphia, Pennsylvania,
Rachmaninoff appeared as composer, conductor, and pianist, presenting most of his master works. (See 1918)

Igor Stravinsky settled in the United States and married his second wife Vera Soudeikine of Bedford,
Massachusetts. Stravinsky held the first performance
of his ballet Jeu de Cartes (Card Play) in New York
City. (See 1925)

The Tolstoy Foundation was established in New York
City by a group of Russian Americans headed by Alexandra
Tolstoy, daughter of the world famous Russian classic
writer Leo Tolstoy. The aim of the foundation was to
assist refugees from Soviet Russia and other countries
under Communist rule in the field of welfare, immigration, integration, employment, etc. The activities
of the foundation soon expanded, and it proved to be
one of the best organized and influential organizations
of the Russian Americans. A semi-annual Newsletter
is the Foundation's well-illustrated publication, reporting on the activities, accomplishments, and needs
of the foundation.

Igor Sikorsky invented the VS-300, the first successful helicopter built in the Western hemisphere. (See
1931)

Gleb Derujinski, noted sculptor, created "Europa and
the Bull," a fountain group displayed at the New York
World's Fair. His versatility was exemplified by three
other groups in the Brookgreen Gardens in South Carolina, "Samson and a Lion," in stone, and "Ecstacy"
and "Diana Hunting," in bronze.

1940   Statistics have recorded that during the last decade
only about 14,000 immigrants have arrived from Russia
to the United States, compared to about 40,000 during
the twenties and about 50,000 at the turn of the twentieth century and its first decade.

April 20. Vladimir Zworykin invented the first electron
microscope. The new microscope was ten feet high,
weighed about 1,000 pounds, and magnified up to 100,000
times. It was described by its inventor at a convention
of the American Philosophical Society held in Philadelphia, Pennsylvania. (See 1938)

Vladimir Nabokov, one of the most original, talented,
and prolific contemporary writers in Russian and Eng-

lish, settled in the United States after already achieving fame for his numerous novels in Russian. During
the following decades he taught Russian language and
literature at Cornell and Harvard universities, but at
the same time did not give up writing. Shortly after
his arrival in the United States, Nabokov published
The Real Life of Sebastian Knight, his first novel in
English.

1941 The pianist Alexander Borovsky settled in the United
States and became professor of music at Boston University. Before coming to the United States, Borovsky
visited several countries and was a soloist with
virtually all major European orchestras.

Anatole Oboukhoff and Vera Nemtchinova, husband and
wife, two noted ballet dancers, settled in the United
States after touring extensively in Europe and gaining
fame. Both became teachers at the School of American
Ballet, New York.

The Hoover Institution of Stanford, California, started publishing The Russian Review, a quarterly covering
several facets of Russia: history, economy, politics,
culture.

The Tolstoy Foundation established the Reed Farm on
seventy-five acres of land near Nyack, New York, later
named the Tolstoy Foundation Center, as a resettlement
place for European refugees and victims of World War
II. This center hosted several thousands of refugees
and presently provides a year-round residence for one
hundred people.

1942 August 22. Michael Fokine, dancer and choreographer,
died in New York City at the age of 62. Among his
latest creations were Paganini, Blue Bird, and Helen
of Troy.

The World Fellowship of Slavical Evangelical Christians
published Evangelskoye Slovo (Gospel World) in Chicago,
Illinois.

Novyj Zhurnal (The New Review) started to appear as a
private quarterly in New York City.

1943 March 28. The world renowned musician Sergei Rachmaninoff died in Beverly Hills, California, at the age of
seventy.

Alexis Romanoff joined the faculty of Harvard University, teaching embriology for the next two decades. He

later became professor emeritus and published several
scholarly books on the subject of avian embriology.

The Russian Orthodox Catholic Church in America was
organized under the jurisdiction of the Moscow (Russia)
patriarchate. It reunited sixty-seven churches with
about 150,000 members.

Natalie Wood, born Natasha Gurdin, well known movie
actress, appeared for the first time in the movie
Happy Land at the age of four. A few years later she
distinguished herself in the movie Tomorrow is Forever.

1945   Igor Youskevitch joined the New York Ballet theater,
winning great critical acclaim during the next decade
as an outstanding classic dancer.

The American Russian Aid Association was founded in
New York City with the aim of helping Russian refugees
in the United States.

Two new Russian publications came into existence:
Nashi Vesti (Our News) issued by the Russian Corps
Combatants, Inc., in New York City, and Strannik
(Pilgrim) published by the Christian Evangelical
Pentacostal Faith of Garfield, New Jersey.

1946   George Balanchine became the artistic director of the
Ballet Society, later known as the New York City Ballet.
Under Balanchine's leadership, New York City Ballet became one of the leading American ballet companies for
the following decades, and Balanchine recorded several
great creations such as Agon, Electronics, Don Quijote,
and many others.

Znamya Rossii (The Banner of Russia) started publication as a monthly organ of Russian independent monarchist
thought dedicated to anti-Communist political views.
It appears in New York City.

1947   A new wave of Russian immigrants came to the United
States. It consisted of former war prisoners, slave
laborers or refugees in Germany during the Second
World War, who refused to return to Russia. It is es-
timated that about 20,000 Russians found asylum in the
United States during the period from 1947 to 1952.

Vladimir Usachevsky, composer, joined the faculty of
Columbia University and made interesting contributions
in the field of electronic music. He perfected an in-
strument capable of transforming recorded music in various ways, producing automatically repeated notes and
diverse dynamic effects.

1948   Victor Seroff, a pianist and biographer of musical
               personalities, published his book Rachmaninoff, devoted
               to the life of the world renowned Russian American mu-
               sician. (See 1943)

1949   Alexander Tcherepnin, composer and pianist, joined the
               faculty of De Paul University of Chicago, Illinois.
               Besides several musical compositions, Tcherepnin is
               credited with adopting a nine-tone scale and applying
               it in several of his instrumental works. He also ela-
               borated a method of rhythmic polyphony.

1950   The Trinity Monastery of Jordanville, New York, started
               to publish the Orthodox Life, devoted to the preserva-
               tion of the traditional Orthodox Christianity, and
               Pravoslavnaia Zhizn (Orthodox Life), describing the
               life of saints and specific features of the Russian
               Orthodox Church outside Russia.

               In the meantime, two other Russian publications came
               into existence in California: Po Stopam Khrista
               (Following the Steps of Christ), issued by the Ortho-
               dox Press of Berkley, California, and Soglasiye (Har-
               mony), a private anti-Communist monthly published in
               Los Angeles.

               The Russian Orthodox Church in Exile formed its own
               synod in the United States and changed its name to
               Russian Orthodox Church Outside Russia. It reunited
               about 50,000 members organized in eighty churches.
               This body constantly refused and never had any con-
               nections with the Moscow (Russia) patriarchate. (See
               1923)

1951   Painter Sergey Rossolovsky came to the United States
               and established himself in Portland, Maine. He soon
               became known as a noted artist in the Russian American
               community through his talented works.

1952   October 28. Michael Rostovtzev died in New Haven,Con-
               necticut, at the age of eighty-two. He distinguished
               himself especially as the director of the Yale Dura-
               Europos expedition, which lasted almost two decades,
               and brought to light very interesting aspects of the
               Hellenistic world.

               St. Vladimir's Orthodox Theological Seminary of Crest-
               wood, New York, started putting out an English quarter-
               ly bearing the title of the Seminary.

               The Orthodox Herald, Inc., of San Antonio, Texas, start-
               ed a monthly publication with the same name featuring
               news and spiritual guidance to the believers of Ortho-

dox faith, as well as religious poetry, recipes for
Russian dishes.

1953   February 14. Igor Stravinsky's opera <u>The</u> <u>Rake's</u> <u>Pro-</u>
<u>gress</u>, based on a text by W. H. Auden and Ch. Kallmar,
was given its American premiere by the New York Metropolitan Opera.

        June. Vladimir Zworykin invented the electronic high-
way system. He demonstrated it for the first time with
a controlled mini car.

        Alexandra Tolstoy, founder of the Tolstoy Foundation
of New York City, published a very interesting biogra-
phy of her father, entitled, <u>Tolstoy</u>: <u>a</u> <u>Life</u> <u>of</u> <u>My</u>
<u>Father</u>. It was followed by another book called <u>The</u>
<u>Tragedy</u> <u>of</u> <u>Tolstoy</u>.

        Sergei Dobrovolsky joined the Rensselaer Polytechnic
Institute of Troy, New York, where he became chairman
of the Department of Economics. He published several
studies on economic statistical facets of the United
States.

1954   <u>Rodniye</u> <u>Dali</u> (Native Vistas) started to be issued as a
monthly by a company with the same name in Los Angeles,
California.

1955   Vladimir Nabokov published his novel <u>Lolita</u>, which
caused a great sensation in literary circles and later
was made into a movie. (See 1940)

        <u>Rossiyskaia</u> <u>Nezavisimost</u> (Russian Independence) started
to appear as a private literary and political magazine
in Brooklyn, New York.

1957   The St. Sergius of Radonezh Russian Orthodox Church
was built at the Tolstoy Foundation Center by architect Vladimir Bush. The church has frescoes decorating
the interior walls, valuable paintings and woodcarvings,
and presents many features of interest in the field of
Russian Orthodox church art.

1958   Nina Berberova, who came to the United States at the
beginning of the fifties, became a professor of Russian
language and literature at Princeton University, New
Jersey, and taught for more than a decade. She distinguished herself as a very fine translator of Russian
works and made contributions to a volume of literary
criticism on Vladimir Nabokov.

        Composer Dimitri Tiomkin of Hollywood, California,

author of the score for the movie <u>The Old Man and the Sea</u>, was awarded an Academy Award. He received the same award for several other successful movie scores, such as <u>The High and the Mighty</u>, <u>High Noon</u>, and <u>The Great Waltz</u>.

The American Society for Russian Naval History and the All-Russian Monarchist Front were established in New York City as two anti-Communist organizations.

At the same time, the Russian Immigrants Association in America started to put out a monthly called <u>Russkoye Delo</u> (The Russian Cause) providing critical analysis of the theory, practice and propaganda of Communism.

1960   Vladimir Zworykin demonstrated the electronic highway system with a standard automobile.

Boris Morkovin of Los Angeles, California, published his book <u>Through the Barriers of Deafness and Isolation</u>. It was the result of several years of work in the field of hearing disorders, and numerous contributions made to specialty journals by Morkovin.

1961   Helen Iswolsky of New York City specialized in Russian language and literature and published her <u>Christ in Russia</u>, considered to be the author's major work. She previously published other books on religious subjects and made contributions to professional journals.

Actress Natalie Wood successfully starred as Maria in the movie adaptation of Leonard Bernstein's <u>West Side Story</u>. She later appeared in several other movies such as <u>Penelope</u>, and <u>Gypsy</u>.

Kyra Petrovskaya, an actress and television singer who came to the United States after the Second World War, published <u>Kyra's Secrets of Russian Cooking</u>. Petrovskaya later published several books for children on mythological subjects.

Serge Zenkovsky of De Land, Florida, specialized in Slavic linguistics and Russian history, and published a book entitled <u>Conversational Russian</u>, followed by <u>Medieval Russia's Epics and Tales</u>.

1962   Olga Andreyev Carlisle of New York City, a grand-daughter of the noted Russian writer Leonid Andreiev, published a book called <u>Voices in the Snow</u>, in which she described her meetings with several prominent Soviet writers, the Nobel prize winner Boris Pasternak being one of them.

Serge Chermayeff of New Haven, Connecticut, became
professor of architecture at Yale University. Chermayeff distinguished himself as an abstract painter with
works exhibited at the Metropolitan Museum of Art and
the Art Institute of Chicago, Illinois.

Vladimir Nabokov published in English a translation of
Alexander Pushkin's Eugene Onegin. The translation
was considered by Nabokov himself "the greatest work
of my life." Pushkin was a great Russian poet, and
his work Eugene Onegin inspired the opera of the same
name by Peter Tchaikovsky.

1963   Sergei Pushkarev of New Haven, Connecticut, a scholar
            specializing in Russian history, published a very in-
            teresting study entitled The Emergence of Modern Russia,
            1801-1917. He also published several other books on
            the same subject.

1964   March 6. Alexander Petrunkevich died at the age of
            eighty-nine in New Haven, Connecticut. He made im-
            portant contributions in the field of invertebrate mor-
            phology and catalogued the spiders of the Western hemis-
            phere.

1967   April. Svetlana Alliluyeva, daughter of I. Stalin,
            the Soviet dictator during the years 1924 to 1953, de-
            fected to the West and established herself in the United
            States, where she was granted political assylum. She
            soon published Twenty Letters to a Friend, a book of
            auto-biographical nature, which became a best seller.
            She also published a second book called A Year Later.

            Victor Petrov joined the faculty of George Washington
            University, Washington, D.C., as a lecturer in geogra-
            phy. He wrote several articles on Soviet and Chinese
            geography and published, among others, the book China:
            Emerging World Power.

            About 200 Russian Orthodox Old Believers, members of
            a sect whose persecution started three centuries ago
            in Russia, came to Alaska and founded their own settle-
            ment Nikolaevsk, named for St. Nicholas, patron of
            their church. This group of Russian expatriates origin-
            ally settled in Oregon, but left this state to shield
            their children from the influence of alcohol, drugs,
            and television, and to raise them in the spirit of their
            religious traditions.

1968   February 10. Pitirim Sorokin died in Winchester,
            Massachusetts, at the age of seventy-nine, leaving
            behind innumerable contributions as a researcher,

Vladimir Petrov, a lecturer and writer, who taught
international affairs for twenty years at the George
Washington University, Washington, D.C., published his
book entitled <u>June 21, 1941</u>: <u>Soviet Historians and
the German Invasion</u>. Petrov made 400 contributions
to different American journals.

The Russian American Youth Theater was founded in New
York City by Tamara Levitskaya, a talented actress and
director, who came to the United States in the fifties.
She concentrated around her several young Russian American talents, developed an interesting repertoire, and
made her theater a success.

1969   Oliver James Lissitzyn, professor of International Law
at Columbia University, New York, published his <u>Cases
and Materials on International Law</u>. He previously published a study on the International Court of Justice,
as well as several contributions to different law journals.

Gleb Derujinsky of New York City was awarded the Allied
Artists Gold Medal of Honor for Sculpture for his work
"Angel of Sorrow" in alabaster.

1970   St. Joseph's School of Brooklyn, New York, revived publication of <u>Podsnezhnik</u> (Snowdrop) featuring stories,
poetry, sketches, humor, and drawings by school students.
The revival took place after an interruption of eleven
years.

June 30. Alexander Kerensky died in New York City at
the age of eighty-nine. (See 1934)

Wassily Leontief, reputed economist, became president
of the American Economic Association. He made several
contributions in the field of economics and won international reputation. (See 1931)

The Russian Orthodox Greek Catholic Church of America
was recognized as a fully independent body by the Moscow
(Russia) patriarchate, and changed its name to the Russian Orthodox Church of America. This body, the largest
of three Russian Orthodox groups in America, reunites
about 600,000 people, organized in 350 churches.

According to the United States Census data, 334,615
Russian Americans declared Russian as their mother
tongue. Russian Americans had at that time thirty-
one publications, twenty-five in their native tongue,
and six in English, with a total circulation of 65,128
copies.

1971   The Census Bureau of the United States issued a study
on self-identification by individuals according to
their origin or descent. Among seven major ethnic
groups, families whose head was Russian lead in median
income of $11,554 a year, and in number of males and
professional and technical jobs.

April 6. Igor Stravinsky died in New York City at the
age of eighty-nine. Stravinsky was very active until
the end of his life. He devoted the last years mostly
to chamber music.

1972   June 18. George Balanchine and his friends at the New
York City Ballet celebrated Stravinsky's birthday in
a week long festival featuring Stravinsky's works.
Stravinsky and Balanchine were close friends for decades, and are viewed as the greatest composer and the
greatest choreographer of our time.

October 26. Igor Sikorsky died in Easton, Connecticut,
at the age of eighty-seven. Besides his outstanding
contributions to the American aviation, Sikorsky was
also an author of books such as The Invisible Encounter,
The Story of the Winged S.

1973   May 5. Nicholas Mordvinoff of Hempton, New Jersey,
died at the age of sixty-two. He was a talented graphic
artist in the field of children's book illustration.

Columbia University, New York City, created a new
chair called Bakhmeteff Professor of Russian Studies
Chair, with M. Raeff to be its first holder. The chair
honors the late Professor B. Bakhmeteff, who established the fund for Russian studies.

1974   The St. Serafimovich Fund of New York City organized
a literary evening to honor the Russian American poet
Ivan Elagin.

The Russian American community of St. Petersburg,
Florida, celebrated the twenty-fifth anniversary of
Mrs. Elena Dolina's artistic activities in the United
States

1975   Kaleriya Fedicheva, a leading ballerina of the Kirov
company of Leningrad, U.S.S.R., left her native country
to join her American husband, a former dancer with the
Maryland Ballet Company.

The Russian American Youth Theater celebrated its
seventh year of its existence. During this period,
the theater presented several plays by Russian classic
and noted Western playrights, and recorded an average

audience of about 250 people per show. (See 1968)

February. New Jersey High School students produced
a taped television program in Russian so effective
that other schools are using it to teach foreign
languages. The program called "Gorki," after the
world famous Russian writer Maxim Gorki, was pat-
terned after Sesame Street television program.

March. The Russian society "Rodina" of Lakewood, New
Jersey, exhibited a collection of paintings and sculp-
tures by noted Russian American artists as well as by
representatives of promising young talents. The first
prize was awarded to Igor Redkin, a nineteen year old
sculptor.

March 10. The noted sculptor Gleb Derujinsky died in
New York City at the age of eighty-six. During the
last years of his life, Derujinsky received the Therese
Richard Award of the Allied Artists of America, the
Anna Hyatt Huntington Award of the American Artists
Professional League, and the Pauline Law Prize. Some
of his works have been acquired by the Metropolitan
Museum of New York City.

April 1. Alexandra Sannikova of New York City, widow
of the late General A. S. Sannikov, celebrated her
100th birthday. She settled in the United States in
1955, studied the United States history, led a very
active life, and to this day she is very vivacious,
preferring the society of young people.

April. S. Chernysh of San Francisco, California, was
promoted to the position of deputy director of the
Californian Institute of Arts, founded by the late
Walt Disney. Chernysh, who completed his higher education in San Francisco, proved to be a very talented
artistic director and teacher on the staff of the institute where he was promoted.

April. Victoriya Feodorova, a leading Soviet movie
star, came to the United States to visit her father
Admiral Jackson R. Tate of Lantana, Florida, for the
first time in her life. During the visit, which was
scheduled for three months, Miss Feodorova married an
American pilot, became a United States resident, and
settled in the United States.

May. In one of its editorials, the Novoye Russkoe
Slovo of New York City voiced its support for Presi-
dent Gerald Ford's plan of resettling about 130,000
South Vietnamese and Cambodian refugees in our country.

May. The Russian American organizations celebrated
the 175th birthday anniversary of Alexander Pushkin,
famous Russian classic poet. The New York Public
Library organized a special exhibit of rare books
and illustrations devoted to or by Pushkin.

May 18. A group of musical students enroled in a
studio conducted by Elena Volonsky, and gave a successful concert in Steinway Hall, New York. Mrs.
Volonsky, a noted music teacher, started the tradition of annual studio concerts in 1958.

July. Russian exilee writer Alexander Solzhenitzyn,
a Nobel Prize winner and one of the most talented
literary figures of our time, made an extensive trip
to the United States visiting several Russian American communities. He received a warm reception from
several Russian American organizations as well as
American academic circles. Solzhenitzyn's works,
ranging from One Day in the Life of Ivan Denisovich,
first book, to Gulag Archipelago, one of the last
writings, were translated and published in the United
States.

September. Alexander Filipov, a favorite ballet dancer of Pittsburgh, Pennsylvania, audiences, born in
Russia and formerly with the Moiseyev Youth Company,
joined the Pittsburgh Ballet Theatre as a principal
dancer. He has been guest artist in residence with
the company for several years, and shared his time
between the American Ballet Theatre, San Francisco
Ballet, and Pittsburgh Ballet Theatre.

The Russian American Congress held its bi-annual
convention in New York City. Among the newly elected
leaders of the organization, there were several representatives of the Russian American younger generation.

The Russian Orthodox Church in America announced that
in a few months it will publish a book entitled Orthodox America: 1794-1976. The book is a tribute to
our country's Bicentennial and reflects the history
and achievements of the Russian Orthodox Church in
America.

DOCUMENTS

GENERAL JOHN BASIL TURCHIN
IN THE CIVIL WAR
1861-1865

John Basil Turchin, born Ivan Vasilyevich
Turchininov, was a Russian immigrant who
came to the United States in 1856, and at
the beginning of the Civil War joined the
19th Illinois Volunteers Regiment. He
served with his regiment in Missouri, Kentucky, and Alabama, took part in the capture of Huntsville and Decatur, and distinguished himself in several other battles.
He was later promoted to the rank of U. S.
Brigadier General. Two of his reports regarding military actions in Chattanooga,
Tennessee, and Ringgold, Georgia, are reproduced.

Source: U. S. War Department. The War
of the Rebellion: A Compilation of the
Official Records of the Union and Con-
federate Armies. Washington, D. C.: G.P.O.,
1880-1902.

No. 157.

*Report of Brig. Gen. John B. Turchin, U. S. Army, commanding
First Brigade.*

HDQRS. FIRST BRIG., THIRD DIV., 14TH ARMY CORPS,
Chattanooga, Tenn., November 30, 1863.

SIR : On the 23d of November, I received orders from the general
commanding the division to move my brigade, consisting of the
Eleventh, Seventeenth, Thirty-first, Thirty-sixth, Eighty-ninth, and
Ninety-second Ohio, and Eighty-second Indiana Volunteer Infantry,
and take position in front of the fortifications in two lines, the right
resting on the Rossville road, the whole division forming an oblique
line with the Fourth Army Corps, then advancing on our left toward
Mission Ridge. Our pickets drove in the pickets of the enemy, and
during that day and the 24th we remained in the same position.

On the 25th, the division was ordered to the left, and at 1 p. m.
took position on the left of the Fourth Army Corps, my brigade
being on the left of Beatty's brigade, Wood's division. As was afterward ascertained, the order was that, at the signal of six guns fired
in succession, the whole line of the center, including our division,
would advance and storm the enemy's position on Mission Ridge,
but the order was brought to our division after the guns were fired,
and some troops of General Sheridan's division on the extreme right
were storming the ridge when we commenced to advance, which was
a little after 3 p. m.

I had the first line (Eleventh, Thirty-sixth, and Ninety-second
Ohio) deployed, and the second line (Seventeenth, Thirty-first, and
Eighty-ninth Ohio and Eighty-second Indiana) in double column

at half distance.   The last two, being small regiments, were formed in one column.   Thick underbrush, Citico Creek, and the rebel rifle-pits impeded considerably the movement of my first line, so that when it had passed thrqugh the woods to the edge of the clearing between the woods and the foot of the ridge, other brigades on my right and left were already crossing the clearing, advancing toward the ridge.   I halted my brigade for a moment, and saw at once that the space between the woods and the ridge was under a cross-fire of powerful rebel batteries on the ridge, on the right and left, and the rebel skirmishers, partly in rifle-pits at the foot of the ridge and partly on the slope of the hill on our front.   I saw General Beatty's brigade on my right and Colonel Van Derveer's brigade on my left, reaching the rebel rifle-pits at the foot of the ridge and dropping down along the ditches, and I decided to cross the clearing at the double-quick.

Both lines moved on a run with a cheer, passed the clearing, reached the rebel rifle-pits at the foot of the ridge, and wavered for a moment, some men dropping down to escape the murderous fire from the enemy's artillery and musketry.   Knowing that men dropping down under fire are very slow to get up and start again, I urged my regiments on, and they again rushed forward and commenced to climb the hill, some of the flank regiments running over the heads of General Beatty's and Colonel Van Derveer's men lying in the rifle-pits on my right and left.

It was impossible to require regularity in the movement up hill. The bravest and the strongest men grouped around the regimental colors, advancing steadily, the balance following irregularly, the head of the column being very narrow and the tail spreading right and left widely.   Three regimental flags of my brigade waved to the breeze almost on the top of the ridge, while the brigades on my right and left were yet lying in the rifle-pits at the foot of the ridge.

Three regiments, the Eleventh, Thirty-first, and Thirty-sixth Ohio, reaching the rebel breastworks on the point A* of the ridge, stormed them, driving the enemy partly down the hill, but mostly along the ridge to the left toward the house B, to which the rebels drove two cannon from the point A, and where there was already one cannon planted, working along the ravine in its front.   This last cannon was captured, but the other two continued to drive down along the ravine.

At the same time, the Ninety-second Ohio and Eighty-second Indiana, with a detachment of the Eighty-ninth Ohio, working their way along the ravine to the left, reached the point C, where two more cannon were captured.

The Seventeenth Ohio having been directed by me in the first place to the right of the point A, drove the rebels from the ridge. charged them down to the woods, and turning to the left to join the other regiments of the brigade struck at the point M, down in the hollow, the two cannon before mentioned, which had passed the house B and were trying to escape down the ravine.   Our men fired at them, and the rebel artillerymen cut the traces and ran away with the horses, leaving the cannon.   These two pieces, with the limbers, were brought on the ridge to the point A, a little before dark, by some men of the Thirty-sixth Ohio sent by me for that purpose, and were left there to the men and officers of Beatty's brigade, Wood's division.

When the point C was taken, our fire obliged the rebels to abandon two pieces of artillery which had been planted at D to fire along the ravine to their front.

The bravest men rushed up the next knob to the left to the point E, and charged on three cannon planted there and supported by rebel infantry.   In the first charge they captured the cannon, but the rebels rallying, drove our men back.   At this time the men of the Second Brigade of our division climbed the hill.   Another charge was made and my men, supported by men of the Second Brigade, took those guns and drove the rebels more to the left.

At this time the Third Brigade reached the top of the hill, and our division took the ridge to the point F, where the fighting continued some time after dark, and where our men built in the night some breastworks.

During the assault and fighting on the ridge my brigade captured alone 7 cannon, and, with the Second Brigade, captured 3 more. Most of them were smooth-bore 6-pounders and Napoleons; 1 or 2 rifled 10-pounders.   Some of the cannon, as the prisoners stated, belonged to Scott's Arkansas [Tennessee] battery.

Besides the cannon, 2 rebel flags were captured—1 regimental flag by the Thirty-first Ohio and 1 battle-flag by the Eleventh Ohio. These flags were subsequently sent, with a separate report, to the general commanding the division.

The fighting continuing on the left, and the regiments being somewhat disorganized, my whole attention was paid to organizing the regiments.   It soon became dark.   I was ordered to bivouac at the point G on the east slope of the ridge, and soon afterward I received orders to leave the ridge, move backward on the western slope, and occupy a position at the foot of the ridge, facing north, to prevent a surprise from the enemy, who still occupied the ground between our division and Sherman's troops at the tunnel.

After leaving the ridge, I do not know what became of the cannon captured by my brigade, but as Beatty's brigade, Wood's division, occupied the hill which we stormed and most of the ground to the left of it, I presume the guns were taken by the regiments of General Beatty's command, and perhaps some by the Second Brigade of 'our division.

The fact was that, reaching the top of the hill, we had more serious work to perform than to count and guard cannon.   The enemy was in strong force on our left, and, until the Second and Third Brigades climbed the hills assigned to them, all our energies were directed to fighting the enemy, and not to grouping and displaying systematically the captured cannon.

The enemy's fire on our right, and with it all danger there, had ceased for a long time, while my brigade was still fighting alone with a powerful enemy on our left.   I moved my brigade down the ridge to the position assigned to it, and bivouacked there during the night

At 7.30 a. m. of the 26th, the brigade was ordered on the ridge again, and at 9.30 a. m. made a reconnaissance to the front to the bridge across Chickamauga River on the road to Chickamauga Station, the general commanding the division being present.   Some 20 prisoners were captured.

At 12 m. the brigade was ordered to move on to the ridge by the Chickamauga Station road.   There we joined the other two brigades, and the division moved on the Ringgold road, bivouacking for the night 6 miles from Ringgold.

On the morning of the 27th, the brigade moved to Ringgold, and was placed in position in the reserve of the division.   We remained

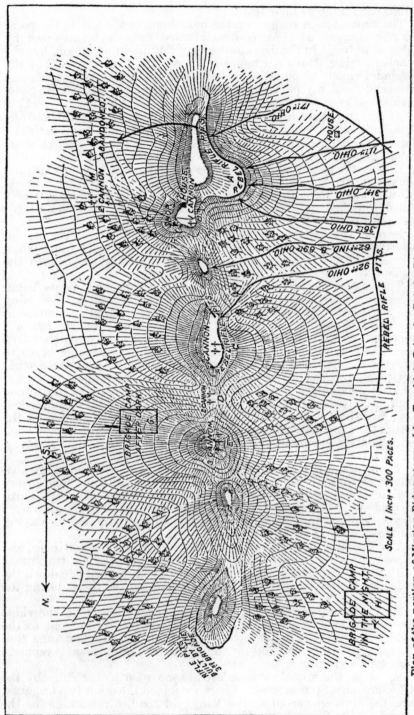

Plan of the portion of Mission Ridge stormed by Turchin's Brigade, Baird's Division, 14th Army Corps, Nov. 25, 1863.

there during the 28th, and on the 29th returned to Chattanooga.

The gallantry of the officers and men of my brigade, during the assault on Mission Ridge, cannot be surpassed. They showed a nerve and bravery that can dare any danger.

I must specially mention Lieutenant-Colonel Putnam, commanding Ninety-second Ohio, wounded in three places; Lieutenant-Colonel Devol, commanding Thirty-sixth Ohio; Lieutenant-Colonel Street, commanding Eleventh Ohio; Lieutenant-Colonel Lister, commanding Thirty-first Ohio, and Colonel Hunter, commanding Eighty-second Indiana, who were all the time at the head of their regiments, and were first on the ridge and in the enemy's works; Lieut. Col. Paul E. Slocum, Eighty-second Indiana; Major Butterfield, Seventeenth Ohio, wounded at the foot of the hill; Captain Jolly, commanding Eighty-ninth Ohio; Captain Grosvenor, commanding the Ninety-second Ohio, after Lieutenant-Colonel Putna was wounded, and Captain Showers, who commanded the Seventeen Ohio after Major Butterfield was wounded.

For an enumeration of all the officers and men who distinguish(themselves, and some of whom suffered severely through their i domitable courage, I beg leave to refer you to the accompanyi reports of the regimental commanders

We have to mourn the loss of some valuable lives, officers a men. The gallant Lieutenant Turner, adjutant of the Ninety-second Ohio, who showed great coolness and intrepidity at the battle of Chickamauga, was mortally wounded on the ridge after the enemy were driven from their works, and has since died. He promised to become an invaluable officer had he lived longer.

It is a pity that the general-in-chief of the army has no right to promote officers and men for bravery on the battle-field. Lieutenant-Colonels Putnam, Devol, Street, and Lister should be made colonels for their gallantry. Many others, officers, sergeants, and privates should be promoted. The bravest men, those who may be called the leaders in every fight, have nothing to show that they are better than others—no national medal, no wreath, no badge, nothing at all.

James B. Bell, color sergeant, Eleventh Ohio, who was wounded in five places before he gave up; Corpl. George Greene and Private H. R. Howard, of the same regiment, who captured the rebel flag; James Walker, private Thirty-first Ohio, who carried the colors after 2 color bearers had fallen, and who captured one of the enemy's flags, and a number of others remarkably brave and gallant, should all be promoted.

In conclusion, I have to recommend to the general commanding the gallantry displayed, on the memorable 25th of November, by the officers of my staff, Captain Curtis, assistant adjutant-general; Captain Hayden, aide-de-camp; Captain Price, inspector, and Captain Dudley, provost-marshal, the latter two acting as aides.

Many prisoners were taken during the assault on Mission Ridge, and also on the 26th and 27th instant, but they were sent to the rear without taking any account of them.

The loss of the brigade was 6 officers and 51 men killed, 11 officers and 211 men wounded, and 4 men missing; total, 17 officers and 266 men.

Inclosed are the official reports and additional statements of the regimental commanders, and a consolidated report of casualties.*

An approximate sketch of the portion of ridge attacked and passed over by my brigade is also forwarded herewith.

I am, sir, very respectfully, your obedient servant,
J. B. TURCHIN,
Brigadier-General, Commanding.
Capt. A. C. McCLURG,
Actg. Asst. Adjt. Gen., 3d Div., 14th Army Corps.

No. 23.

Report of Brig. Gen. John B. Turchin, U. S. Army, commanding
First Brigade, Third Division.

HDQRS. FIRST BRIG., THIRD DIV., 14TH ARMY CORPS,
Ringgold, Ga., March 1, 1864.

SIR : I have the honor to report that on the 22d day of February, 1864, my brigade, consisting of the Eleventh, Eighty-ninth, and Ninety-second Ohio, and Eighty-second Indiana Volunteer Infantry, in all 1,180 men, marched from Chattanooga to Ringgold, Ga., and encamped with the Second Brigade of our division.

On the 23d, we passed Ringgold and camped 2 miles beyond the gap at the Rock [Stone] Church.

On the 24th, the division moved to Terrill's house and camped there.

On the 25th. at 3 a. m., the division moved across the country to the left, and joined General Cruft's command on the Cleveland and Dalton road. Forming on the right of General Cruft's we advanced along the valley east of Rocky Face Ridge, my brigade being formed in two lines, three regiments in one line and one in reserve, the Second Brigade being on my left.

When the Eleventh Regiment Ohio Volunteers, moving in column on the road, approached the point A, the enemy opened with two pieces of artillery posted on the left of the grove C. Their range was so accurate that the first shell wounded 5 of our men.

The Eleventh Ohio Volunteers deployed in the field, the Ninety-second Ohio Volunteers in the thicket on the left; the Eighty-second Indiana Volunteers formed in the woods behind and to the right of the Eleventh Ohio Volunteers, and the Eighty-ninth Ohio Volunteers was sent along the foot of the ridge across the ravine toward the log house B. Besides the line of skirmishers on our front (two companies from each of the two regiments) I sent two companies from the Eleventh Ohio Volunteers and one company from each of the other regiments, in all five companies, on the slope and to the top of the ridge to protect our right from the enfilading fire of the enemy's sharpshooters, posted on the slope of the ridge.

The ridge being very steep, a great many sharp and short spurs from it formed abrupt ravines, steep hills, and sometimes isolated knolls, filling the side of the valley at the foot of the ridge, and forming when occupied by the enemy a series of impregnable positions.

After some skirmishing with the enemy occupying the knoll and grove C, four pieces of Captain Simonson's (Indiana) battery, forming on the right of the Eleventh Ohio Volunteers, shelled the grove for a half hour, and the enemy ceased firing.

The Eighty-ninth Ohio Volunteers, occupying the knob in front of the log-house, reported that the enemy were strong in their front. Reports from the companies on the slope of the ridge corroborated the report of the Eighty-ninth Ohio Volunteers, and Captain Layman, of the Eleventh Ohio Volunteers, sent me information from the top of the ridge that at least a division of the enemy was lying on our front.

General Palmer wished me to charge and take possession of the grove C. I reported to him that I had information from the different regiments that the enemy was too strong on my front, and that it would be dangerous to charge to the left while my flank was unprotected.

About noon General Baird directed my whole brigade to the right, and it was formed with the Eleventh Ohio Volunteers at the foot of the ridge, the Eighty-ninth Ohio and Eighty-second Indiana Volunteers, on the knoll D, called Sugar Loaf Point, and the Ninety-second Ohio Volunteers at the log-house.

While at the log-house General Whipple, chief of staff of Department of the Cumberland, urged me to charge the grove C, supposing that it was the key of the position, and that if taken it would open the gap beyond Buzzard Roost where General Davis' column was stopped by the enemy.

Before directing my command to charge the grove C, which was to our left, I ordered the Eleventh Regiment Ohio Volunteers, supported by the Ninety-second Ohio Volunteers, to move to the front to provoke the enemy and oblige him to show his force. The regiment moved down the ravine and commenced to climb the opposite hill, but the enemy in front and on the flank opened such a murderous fire that the regiment was broken in the twinkling of an eye. The enemy pursuing, several companies of the Ninety-second Ohio Volunteers broke also, but Captain Grosvenor of that regiment, with about 60 men, charged the scattering enemy and drove them back to their position.

At the same time the enemy charged the Eighty-ninth Ohio and Eighty-second Indiana Volunteers, posted on the knoll D, but were repulsed and followed by our men down the slope into the ravine and up the hill for some distance, when they, being re-enforced, covered our advancing men with volleys and drove them back. We retained our position, but in ten minutes lost 86 men and Lieutenant-Colonel Slocum, commanding Eighty-second Indiana Volunteers, who was very dangerously wounded.

This attempt to advance showed clearly what danger was in store not only for my brigade but the whole division. If I had moved to the left and attacked the grove C the enemy would have taken me in flank, thrown me on the Second Brigade in disorder, and attacked the Second Brigade in flank also.

Two regiments of the Third Brigade were now moved to support me on the right. After our short but sharp fighting all was quiet on our front until night, we not daring to advance and the enemy quietly waiting.

According to the information from the officers posted on the ridge, it appears that the enemy occupied in strong force the hills at the foot of the ridge on my front and the groves on the ridge east of us in General Cruft's front, posting some cavalry in the open valley between these two outstretched fists as a bait for our advance, while his main reserves were massed back in the open fields ready to support the right or left, or be hurled on the center. About a division.

posted in three lines, with a strong battery on their right, supported by another line of infantry, was on our front, and in action only the first line of rebel infantry participated.

We paid unfortunately for our success in discovering the "bear in his den" by a loss of 9 killed and 78 wounded, among the latter Lieut. Col. Paul E. Slocum.

Among the officers who distinguished themselves in our short but severe encounter I must mention Capt. Edward Grosvenor, of the Ninety-second Ohio Volunteers, who, while several companies of that regiment broke, with 28 men of his own and 20 men of other companies, rushed forward to the support of the Eleventh Ohio Volunteers, charged on the enemy scattering in pursuit of our men, drove them back, and retained his position in the front during the whole afternoon.

I especially commend him to the favorable consideration of the general commanding the department, as an officer who showed his bravery and coolness in the battles of Chickamauga and Mission Ridge, leading his regiment in the latter battle after Lieutenant-Colonel Putnam was wounded. and now showing his pluck again so conspicuously and opportunely. I earnestly recommend him for promotion.

Among the enlisted men the color bearers of the regiments behaved bravely. They deserve great credit for their gallantry.

The small size of the régiments and brigades of our army mix up our ideas about their capacities. Forgetting to ascertain the number of men, a brigade is assigned sometimes to a duty requiring a division. This may lead often to very grave consequences.

My brigade in this fight, excluding the nine companies that acted as skirmishers, consisted of not more than 800 men, who fought on the position—merely a common regiment.

An approximate sketch* of the position on our front and right is annexed. The reports of the regimental commanders, and a consolidated list of casualties, are inclosed.

I am, sir, very respectfully, your obedient servant,

J. B. TURCHIN,
Brigadier-General, Commanding.

Maj. JAMES A. LOWRIE,
Assistant Adjutant-General.

—

Casualties of the First Brigade, Third Division, Fourteenth Army Corps, February 25, 1864.

Regiment.	Killed.		Wounded.		Total.		Aggregate.
	Officers.	Men.	Officers.	Men.	Officers.	Men.	
82d Indiana		3	2	21	2	24	26
11th Ohio		1		24		25	25
89th Ohio		2		11		13	13
92d Ohio		4		19		23	23
Total		10	2	75	2	85	87

J. B. TURCHIN,
Brigadier-General, Commanding.

HDQRS. 1ST BRIG., 3D DIV.. 14TH A. C.,
Ringgold, Ga., March 1, 1864.

THE ALASKA PURCHASE
1867

On March 30, 1867 Russia and the United States concluded a convention for the cessation of Alaska, a Russian possession in North America, to the United States for the amount of 7,200,000 dollars paid in gold. According to the convention, all Russian Orthodox churches built in Alaska remained the property of the church members, and the Russians who chose to remain under American administration were given full privileges as United States citizens. The text of the convention is reproduced below.

Source: Malloy, William M. comp. U. S. Treaties. Treaties, Conventions, International Acts, Protocols and Agreements Between the United States of America and Other Powers, 1776-1937. Washington, D. C.: G.P.O., 1910-38, vol. II, p. 1521 ff.

CONVENTION FOR THE CESSION OF THE RUSSIAN POSSESSIONS IN NORTH AMERICA TO THE UNITED STATES Concluded March 30, 1867. Ratifications exchanged at Washington, June 20, 1867. Proclaimed June 20, 1867.

... ART. I. ... His Majesty the Emperor of all the Russias agrees to cede to the United States, by this Convention, immediately upon the exchange of the ratifications thereof, all the territory and dominion now possessed by his said Majesty on the continent of America and in the adjacent islands, the same being contained within the geographical limits herein set forth, to wit: The eastern limit is the line of demarcation between the Russian and the British possessions in North America, as established by the convention between Russia and Great Britain, of February 28—16, 1825, and described in Articles III. and IV. of said convention, in the following terms: ...

" 'IV. With reference to the line of demarcation laid down in the preceding article, it is understood—

" '1st. That the island called Prince of Wales Island shall belong wholly to Russia,' ...

" '2d. That whenever the summit of the mountains which extend in a direction parallel to the coast from the 56th degree of north latitude to the point of intersection of the 141st degree of west longitude shall prove to be at the distance of more than ten marine leagues from the ocean, the limit between the British possessions and the line of coast which is to belong to Russia as above mentioned, (that is to say, the limit to the possessions ceded by this convention,) shall be formed by a line parallel to the winding of the coast, and which shall never exceed the distance of ten marine leagues therefrom.' " ...

ART. II. ... In the cession of territory and dominion made by the preceding article are included the right of property in all public lots and squares, vacant lands, and all public buildings, fortifications, barracks, and other edifices which are not private individual property. It is, however, understood and agreed, that the churches which have been built in the ceded territory by the Russian Government, shall remain the property of such members of the Greek Oriental Church resident in the territory as may choose to worship therein. . . .

ART. III. . . . The inhabitants of the ceded territory, according to their choice, reserving their natural allegiance, may return to Russia within three years; but, if they should prefer to remain in the ceded territory, they, with the exception of uncivilized native tribes, shall be admitted to the enjoyment of all the rights, advantages, and immunities of citizens of the United States, and shall be maintained and protected in the free enjoyment of their liberty, property, and religion. The uncivilized tribes will be subject to such laws and regulations as the United States may from time to time adopt in regard to aboriginal tribes of that country. . . .

ART. VI. In consideration of the cession aforesaid, the United States agree to pay at the Treasury in Washington . . . seven million two hundred thousand dollars in gold. . . .

FORT ROSS AND THE RUSSIANS
1893

Fort Ross, the first Russian settlement
in California, located in Sonoma county,
was established in 1812 and abandoned in
1841. The Russian settlers returned to
Alaska, where they initially resided, and
were sent to California by Alexander Baranof, the manager of the Russian-American
Company at that time. At the end of the
nineteenth century, Charles S. Greene visited Fort Ross and published a very informative article regarding the history
of Fort Ross and its subsequent evolution.

Source: Overland Monthly, vol. XXII, section 2 (July 1893), pp. 1-15.

TRADITIONS and ivy are said to grow well in but one place on the Atlantic seaboard of this country, at Newport. On the West Coast it is quite as diffi-cult to find the combination. Fort Ross alone seems to fill it well. Even there the ivy is not very abundant, though it covers the side of the old hotel, and creeps into one of the bed-rooms and festoons its mantelpiece. But the traditions are abundant enough. All around are evidences of a history that had its close half a century ago. All the people have stories to tell of the ancient days. There is even a "haunted chamber," where the ghosts of the past walk at night. The smallest toddler of the group of children there, a little fellow of only three years, will pick up one of the rusty hand-wrought spikes of curious shape that are part of the soil in places, and tell you that "the 'Ooshians made that." Of course traditions that had their source all with-in the nineteenth century are not ven-erable by any but Californian standards, yet they nevertheless impress the visitor of today as venerable.

The bastions of the old fort are fast falling to decay. The roof of one is gone, and of the other will hardly-stand more than two or three winters more. Even the solid redwood logs of the structure itself are rotted so that a cane may be thrust into their substance wherever it is sapwood, though the heartwood still is sound. Thus the bas-tions bow a little more each year to the southward, where the fierce gales sweep in from the ocean, and by-and-by will fall. And well they may ; for they have overreached their three score years and ten, which is pretty well for wood-en buildings that, so far as appears, never had a touch of paint.

But these are the chief marks still left of a settlement that might have had far-reaching effects on California's history. On this spot for thirty years the Russians kept up the best garri-soned, best armed, and strongest for-tress in California.

A slight sketch of the history of the settlement (drawn chiefly from Hittell and Bancroft as authorities, with addi-tion of some reminiscences of General

John Bidwell) will be necessary to make the description of it as it is now best understood.

The Spaniards by the opening of the present century had possession of all of California as far north as San Francisco, and their familiar system of the mission and the presidio, with its resulting pueblo, was in more or less prosperous working from Baja California to San Francisco. They knew that Russian settlements had been made in the extreme North,—that Hudson Bay men and the representatives of the new and aggressive American Republic were growing unpleasantly numerous on their coasts and northern boundaries, and strict laws were made to enforce Spain's well-known colonial policy, forbidding trade and intercourse with foreign vessels, except such succor in distress as humanity demanded.

But the English, Russians, and Americans, were not easily kept at arm's length, especially the last two. The Yankee traders were ubiquitous in their handy vessels, and wherever there were furs to be taken the Russians were bound to go. But that meant far down the coast, for the valuable sea otter in those days was found in large numbers in San Francisco Bay and yet farther south, while many fur seals were taken on the Farallones.

Ever since 1741 when Bering discovered the coast, Russian attention had been given to Northwest America, and by 1745 permanent settlements had been made there. These settlements were frequently hostile to each other and to new arrivals, and were also engaged many times in wars of extermination with the natives, but by 1785 they had begun to consolidate, and in 1799 had been formed the great Imperial Russian-American Fur Company that was to rule until Russia gave up all claims on American soil in 1868. The Czar and others of the royal family

were interested in this company. Yet it was strictly a commercial enterprise, and the hold it got on its territories, however extensive and permanent, had but little of political significance and was readily relinquished for commercial reasons. Politica supremacy in America was no part of the famous policy of Peter the Great. This, it seems to me, must be borne in mind, to understand the whole course of Russian dealings in America,—at Fort Ross included.

But Yankee enterprise was needed to point out the southern way to Baránof in his Sitka castle. In 1803 one Captain O'Cain arrived at Sitka, and bargained with the company to take a party of their Kodiak otter hunters and their bidarkas to southern waters, there to hunt for furs on shares. This trip proved successful, and similar trips were made by a vessel or two each year until 1815. These bidarkas were skin boats, commonly holding only one man, as those shown in the sketch, but made also with two openings ; and still larger craft bore the same name, for Payeras tells how he and the Imperial Mexican Commissionado, Canonigo Fernandez, were later rowed from Ross to Bodega in a bidarka. It is a possible conjecture, however, that the good prelate mistook the name, for he was not much used to boats and was wofully seasick on this trip. At any rate, that carried fifteen oarsmen. The otter hurting was probably done in the smaller boats.

But the Sitka people were not of the sort to allow men of another nation to do for them what they could do themselves, and the visit of the Imperial Chamberlain Resanoff to San Francisco in 1806, celebrated for its tragic tale of love, had put them still further in possession of the facts of the situation. They knew that the reserve of the Spaniards, was not absolutely impregnable, and so a bold move was undertaken. In 1808 Ivan Kuskof, Baranof's lieutenant, started on a preliminary voyage of observation, and early in 1809 dropped anchor in Bodega Bay. Then, and on a second voyage in 1811, he made explorations of the neighboring territory, and was specially pleased with a spot about twenty miles up the coast from Bodega Bay, where a little open plateau of good soil overlooked the sea, cut off from the surrounding conntry in several directions by deep gulches, so that it was easy of defense. Moreover, it had pasturage, timber, running water, and what its inhabitants to this dav claim is "the best climate on the Coast." To this place, thenceforth to be called Fort Ross, he acquired a semblance of title for his company by purchase from the Indians, paying, according to Bancroft's citation from Payeras, stout old prefect of missions, who was grieved and scandalized at this occupation of Spanish soil by foreign heretics, "three blankets, three pairs of breeches, two axes, three hoes, and some beads."

The actual settlement was made in 1812, when Kuskof arrived on the Chirikof with ninety-five Russians, and forty bidarkas with two Aleuts to man each bidarka. They arrived in March or April, and by September had the fort and village completed.

The motive of the Russians in making the settlement, beside the fur-taking already mentioned, was to provide a base of supplies for the Sitka colony. I quote a paragraph from an article in the San Francisco *Times*, of Jan. 16, 1869, by Father Agapius Honcharenko, a Russian refugee in California, who in his "Little Ukrainia" settlement, near Haywards, has given Russian matters much attention.

One of the greatest troubles of Baránof was keeping the colonies supplied with subsistence, and the actual necessities of life. The connections of the colonies with Russia were from the first through Siberia. Frequent shipwrecks made these connections irregular, and placed the colonies in a critical position. To insure all cf the articles of first neces-

sity, and from the difficulty of raising breadstuffs on the islands, Baránof used all possible means to secure firm connections with Manilla, the Philippine Islands, the Sandwich Islands, and at last with California; where he and Kuskof established a colony in the territory belonging to the Spanish government. This was called Fort Ross. The stream running through a certain portion of the land occupied is to this day known by the name of Russian River.

Favoring the Russian plans also was the condition of the Spanish colonies then, and for the ten or twelve years following the settlement, and the general upheaval in Europe and on the eastern shores of America. In this same year of 1812 began the revolts that were not to cease till Spain's dominion on the continent of America was entirely overthrown. The California settlements were not actively engaged in any of these hostilities, but as a result of them the supply ships failed to arrive, and the Spanish troops at the presidios were unpaid, and had to depend on the products of the mission industries, dealt out to them rather grudgingly by the friars. In this way they were in no condition to undertake to dislodge these intruders on Spanish soil, however firmly their governors might be convinced that Ross was in California, which they claimed extended to the Straits of Fuca, while the Russians then or afterward in the controversies were apt to claim that the Spanish title, based on the discovery by Columbus, extended no farther north than San Francisco, the bounds of actual occupation, and the territory north of that was unoccupied land under the general title of New Albion, given it by Drake.

And there was still another reason for friendliness between Russian and Spaniard, — each had what the other eagerly desired. The Russians wanted the Californian wheat and furs, and had to exchange for them many articles of wood, iron, and leather, made by their mechanics at Sitka and Ross, that the Spanish could not get from the disturbed mother country, and were far too easy-going to make for themselves. The bells in certain mission churches were cast at Sitka, and the Russian wrought iron, both from Sitka and Ross, was much desired. When the Aleutian bidarkas first came boldly into San Francisco Bay, the authorities at the Presidio had not a single boat with which to pursue and bring to terms these daring poachers. The only resource was to guard the springs, so that no fresh water could be obtained. Later several boats built at Ross were sold to the San Franciscans. Indeed, the activity of the Russians and those they ruled seemed marvelous and unexplainable to the Spaniards.

Thus there were nearly every year several ships that came from Sitka and Ross to San Francisco, bringing merchandise and carrying away for the North cargoes of wheat; and this traffic, though entirely illegal, and done against the formal protests of the Spanish governors, was no whit the less profitable, especially in the early years of the settlement. Later too, after the San Rafael settlement had been made, no little of this trade went on by land.

Nearly every year some formal complaint was sent by the Spanish, and later by the Mexican, authorities, to the Russians, that they were occupying soil that did not belong to them, warning them to depart, demanding to know by what authority they did these things.

To this Kuskof gave no satisfactory reply, feigning not to understand as long as he could, and when the "no sabee" ruse availed no longer, saying that he was but a subordinate, and but did as he was instructed; that they must go to Baránof. No better results followed an appeal to Sitka; for Baránof in turn referred to the home government at St. Petersburg, and so the farce was re-enacted each year. The Spanish governor gravely reported these matters to the viceroy, with an estimate of the number of troops, infantry and artillery, necessary to dislodge the Russians, a number never forthcoming. It is amusing to read of this mild and almost kindly controversy, that interfered not at all with the trade and friendly intercourse here on this sequestered slope; while the mother countries of both these colonies, and all the civilized world beside, were engaged in the throes of the Napoleonic wars, the war of 1812, and the Spanish-American revolutions.

And truly the task of trying to capture Fort Ross was not an alluring one, —especially to the Spanish forces in California, where the comandante at the San Francisco Presidio had sometimes to send to an incoming foreign ship to borrow the powder before he could return her salute. Its stout redwood logs would stop anything less than a cannon ball. It was mounted with some forty guns when fully armed, and there was beside an abundant supply of small arms. The discipline was always very strict. Sentinels guarded its sally port, and there were from two to four hundred men at the settlement, all more or less trained as soldiers. So the strong walls of Fort Ross gave it peace, and never faced civilized foe; though Alvarado speaks of an easily repulsed attack by a Sotoyome chief, soon after its founding. Yet, most unaccountably, bullets have been dug out of its timbers,—one of them is in the museum of the Society of California Pioneers at San Francisco,—and the proprietor of the hotel at Ross showed me a three-inch cannon bal , and assured me that it was cut out from the inner wall of one of the bastions, having passed entirely through the opposite wall. Possibly these may have been fired at the fort by the Russians themselves, in testing its strength, for there is no record that even a "pirate vessel warping down" ever took a shot at it. But the strength of the fort and its strict discipline had another purpose than to resist attack by the Spaniards, or the neighboring Indians, or any foreign foe. It was largely to keep internal peace. Beside the governor and a few Russian officers, most of the inhabitants of Ross were Aleuts and Siberians, often convicts. To keep these in awe required all of Kuskof's sternness.

Kuskof, governor for the first nine years of the colony, is the man who, of all the Russians at Ross, has most fixed his personality in memory. The Spaniards called him " Pie de Palou," on account of his wooden leg; and he seems to have been a doughty, irascible, but honest old fellow, who entertained well guests of high degree, astonishing them with the appliances of civilization in this wilderness, but who ruled those under him with an iron hand.

The buildings of the fort, all of them constructed by him, are monuments to his executive ability and military exactness, though he was himself a merchant, and not a professional soldier. "Time was no object to those old Russians," one of the present inhabitants told me, speaking of their handiwork. All the woodwork of the fort was made of hand-hewn logs and planks. An ax similar to a broadax was used for both felling and hewing, and their skill with it was wonderful. The logs of the bastions fit together at the corners, where undecayed, so closely that a pen-knife blade can hardly be inserted between them after all these years, and the surfaces are still smooth. Great solidity marks all their work. The building that was the governor's house, now part of the hotel, has logs in its attic that I judged to be eighteen inches in diameter, and forty or fifty feet long. The chimney and fireplace are made entirely of hewn granite slabs, finely surfaced, and fitting together with great exactness. The metal work all over the

place is still largely their hand-wrought iron. A good example of it is in the hinges of the old sally port, (p. 5,) still standing.

There seems to be but one sketch extant of the Fort Ross of early days, that drawn by Duhaut Cilly, a Frenchman, who spent three days at the fort in 1828. This he published in a book of his travels A sketch from a copy of this plate I am able to give (p. 4,) by the kindness of Mr. Call, who now owns the land on which the fort stands. The work itself is to be found in the Bancroft Library.

Four ships, that is to say, schooners and brigs of 160 and 200 tons, were built at Ross, and at least one at Bodega, and this work, with the agricultural operations and all the trades carried on, made the place such a hive of industry that it is no wonder the Spaniards were astonished. And yet, strange to say, the venture as a whole proved unprofitable after a few years. The ships did not compare well in durability with those made of more seasoned and better woods, there were years of crop failure from the rust caused by the damp sea fogs. The Yankee traders brought manufactured goods that undersold the products of the artisans at Fort Ross. and the fur-bearing animals were soon exterminated. In addition to these things, the Mexican authorities continually grew more jealous of foreigners, and though less jealous of the Russians than of English or Americans, still they came again and again with their demand that the Russians evacuate their territory. Now, it is not to be supposed that the Russians feared Mexico. It does not even appear that they ever really expected an attack, and they would hardly have been moved much if they had. Negotiations begun for the cession by Mexico of the territory were rather hampered by the fact that Russia had not then acknowledged Mexican independence. But the game was no longer worth the candle, and orders were given to sell the property and abandon Fort Ross.

A long time before the final abandonment it had been the custom to send back to Sitka by each vessel some of the Kodiak huntsmen, who had been thrown out of employment by the failure of the otter and fur seal. There had been maintained on the Farallones, all through the time that Fort Ross was occupied, a station of Aleuts under a Russian officer. The purpose of this colony, beside fur hunting, was to capture seals and gulls, and dry them for use by the Aleuts at Ross, who preferred seal meat to the venison and bear meat of the mainland, to say nothing of beef or mutton. This station on the Farallones was given up in 1840. There are to this day certain ruined stone huts on the South Farallon, that are called by the light keepers "the Russian houses," though doubt is cast on the matter by some persons, who think that these houses were built by the egg company in later years. An inspection of them casts little light on the matter, but the solidity of the work at Ross, and everywhere that the Russians went, seems to make it probable that they would not have occupied the island twenty-eight years without leaving some traces.

For more than a year negotiations were carried on with Vallejo at San Francisco, regarding the sale of the property; but the stubborn refusal of the Mexicans to consider the buildings, "built on their land with their timber," in fixing the price made this bargaining fruitless, and another purchaser was found in Captain Sutter. He had arrived in California in 1839, from the Sandwich Islands, and had at once established himself at New Helvetia (forerunner of Sacramento), but had not yet built the famous Sutter's Fort. It is quite possible that he had his own fort

in mind in this purchase, for he used the guns to arm it. One of them, a brass four pounder, he afterwards presented to the San Francisco Society of California Pioneers, after it had seen service in the southern campaigns. Sutter's Fort also, though of a different material (adobe), is much like Fort Ross in general plan, a square stockade with a bastion at each end of one of its diagonals.

For $31,000, or rather, for his promise to pay that amount in installments in the absence of sufficient money, Sutter was given all and sundry the properties that the Russians could not remove,—the fort buildings, 41 cannon, 70 stand of flint lock muskets (these he declared, on examination, to be some of those thrown away by Napoleon's troops in the flight from Moscow), 2000 cattle, 1000 horses, 1000 sheep, and a long inventory beside.

He sent John Bidwell to take possession of his new property for him. Bidwell arrived in the first week in January, 1842, but unfortunately the Russians had all sailed away (Bancroft says on January 1, 1842) before he arrived, and so the historian is deprived of the testimony of General Bidwell's strong and clear memory as to what manner of men they were.

But of the Fort as they left it and the life of the days that followed immediately on their going, no better picture can be gained than by a talk with General Bidwell.

He made his home most of the time at Bodega, five miles inland from Bodega Bay, at a place where the Russians had quite a settlement because the wheat lands were better there. There were a dozen houses and two threshing floors. These were made of three-inch planks, were circular in shape, and about one hundred feet in diameter. The grain was trampled out on them by horses, just as the Californians did on their earthen threshing floors.

On the Russian River, not far from Bodega, was the ranch and vineyard of Don Jorge, a Russian of means and scientific attainments, who outstayed his compatriots.

The trip up the coast from Bodega to Ross was a most interesting one of about twenty miles by road. The most exciting part of it was the crossing of the Slavianka (the Russian name for Russian River) on the sand-bar that the ocean waves washed up at its mouth. This was a matter of no little danger, as the bar often shifted and was full of quicksands. Two or three people generally went together, ready with riatas, to help each other in case of need.

Another excitement of the road was the danger of meeting grizzly bears, which at that time were very numerous. There was one little barranca that the road skirted, where in the springtime it was no uncommon thing to look down and see the backs of four or five grizzlies in the deep clover that they like to feed on in that season.

Whales are not uncommonly washed ashore, dead, on that coast, and a dead whale was sure to attract the grizzlies. The Mexicans said a grizzly could smell a whale one hundred miles. At any rate, on the road skirting the ocean it was necessary to be cautious in approaching a dead whale.

The Indians around Fort Ross at that time spoke Russian, beside their own dialect, and knew but little Spanish. It was some time before it was easy to communicate with them. Bancroft speaks of the many Indians showing a mixture of Russian blood.

There was plenty to eat at the Ross of those days, and it is no wonder that the Russians disliked to leave it for the Sitka fare. Grizzly meat, antelopes, ducks, geese, sand-hill cranes, as well as beef, veal, pork, and mutton, were plentiful. Trout were numerous, and salmon crowded the little streams in spawning time. There was an abundance of wild strawberries and huckleberries, and the orchards yielded apples, peaches, and grapes. Bidwell recalls the making of three barrels of cider that first year.

The large orchard, of some two hundred apple trees, is still in bearing on a pretty sheltered slope about a mile northeast of the Fort. The apples are mostly small, for the trees have been neglected, and are covered with "old man moss"; but some are of good size and flavor still. It is said that this orchard was used as a park by the Russian officers and their wives, and was planted with flowers and kept in good order. A plank fence eight feet high surrounded it, (and is still standing in places,) to keep out the Indians and Aleuts. It certainly is a delightful spot, sheltered by the redwoods to the east and north, and overlooking the Fort and the ocean beyond.

In 1842 the old windmill was still standing north of the Fort, a low, strong building, with a log sixty feet long as a sail axis, that a crowd of men could take hold of to push around to the proper angle to the wind. This building has since disappeared, but one of the great burr stones is standing in the hotel yard, and is pointed out as "the millstone that killed the beautiful Russian girl." I inquired how it happened, but got no more satisfactory reply than, "O, she got tangled up in it somehow."

And this brings us again to the Fort Ross of today, already spoken of on many points. I visited it in April, this year. The start is made at eight o'clock in the morning from San Francisco, and Fort Ross is reached at about six in the evening of the same day. First the boat to Sausalito, then by train to the pleasant resort of Cazadero, at one o'clock, — where the road ends. Here we were to take the stage. I paid for our party, and asked for the tickets.

"We don't give tickets, but I've put you on the waybill."

Thus made freight of, we took the stage, the ladies up beside the driver, who proved to be a merry fellow, and told them stories that made them laugh, and stories that made them thrill a bit, especially the one of the robbers that held up the stage at the Bend of the Cañon, when "the big fellow with the mask and shotgun started out from behind that tree,— right there!"

The day had been almost rainy when we left San Francisco, and all the way there were dashes of Scotch mist till late in the afternoon, but this only freshened up all the vegetation to wonderful brilliancy close at hand, shading off into soft grays and blues in the distance that were unspeakably beautiful.

It is with great humility that I try to speak of that ride in the fresh new foliage of the California April,— of the marvelous diversity and wonderful delicacy of the countless shades of green, of the beauty and variety of the wild flowers, and of the perfect pictures presented at each new turn of the road. It was hard to tell on the steep grades on the mountain side whether it was better to look at the bank close at hand on the left, and see the flowers,— iris, yellow violets, trilliums, scarlet larkspurs, saxifrage, and nemophilæ, the dainty ferns, maidenhair and gold back, and the little redwood trees two inches high,— or to look away into the cañon at the right, and see the great redwoods two hundred feet high and the stately convocations of many forest trees, where even the madroño had to stand up straight and tall, reaching upward toward the light that sifted through the branches,— and away beyond to the opposite sides of the cañon, even down the cañon in one clear time making out the great blue bulk of Mt. St. Helen, dim in the mist. That mountain, by the way, bears the name given it by the Russians.

It was about five o'clock when we reached Sea View, a little wayside tavern and postoffice, where the stage road climbs out on the ridge of the hills over Fort Ross and allows a glimpse of the ocean. There we transferred to a private team sent from the Fort and driven by one of the good natured brothers that lease the hotel. We were glad to get out of the stage, for though our eyes had been delighted the whole way, our bones had been sadly racked, as the four horses dragged the mud wagon through rather than over the heavy road, when the wheels sank in up to the hubs in many of the spring-holes.

Yet the ride down to the Fort, three and a half miles, was worse in some respects; for the pitch is very steep, and it seemed as though the heavy jolts would throw us out on the horses' backs. But there was beauty enough here, too. The great ocean lay before us, the redwood trees were about us, the little pines were making Christmas trees of themselves with tiny tapers of light green needles at the end of every bough, and the girls were wild with delight over the beautiful columbines and ferns. And at each turn of the winding road we could see Fort Ross, our goal, growing nearer and still nearer.

We reached it at about seven o'clock and received the proverbial warm welcome of an inn by being surrounded by a group of chattering children, each struggling to get possession of something of our baggage to carry in. Supper followed, and soon to bed, hardly waiting to admire the great stone fireplace in the living-room of the hotel, a monument of Russian skill. Not even the shades of the ghost chamber, where the girls were put, could keep awake travelers so tired.

The days passed only too quickly, crowded full of things to do and see. The most interesting objects are the bastions of the Fort, and the chapel. The condition of the bastions I have spoken of already, and one of my companions, who had been there the year before, remarked sadly on the effects of the storms of one winter on the old watch towers. In the roofless bastion to the south there are a pair of interesting old cannon wheels, wooden, half a foot thick, a foot and a half in diameter, and bound with iron. There is little else left in the structure. The floor of the second story and the staircase are indicated by only a few crumbling beams. The north bastion still has a roof and a part of the flooring, but these will not last long. This bastion is used as a shelter for an unsavory lot of black pigs.

The old bastions have eight sides, and this point is one that I can settle by authority. Bancroft speaks of them as hexagonal, while Hittell correctly says octagonal. A sketch plan made while at Fort Ross showed eight sides, and that was my clear recollection as well, but when I mentioned Bancroft's error to the artists that had been at the Fort with me, they declared positively and independently that there were but six sides. Mr. Fenn's drawing in the *Century* for Nov. '90, showed four sides, while one in *Harper's* a year or two earlier, showed but three. I then questioned four other persons who had seen the buildings, and the responses were equally divided. One of these that said eight, found a photograph, and was shaken by it in her belief, and sent it to me to prove that after all we were wrong. Meanwhile a letter had been written to the Fort to ask for positive testimony, and received the reply that eight was right.

It surely is very deceptive to look at, for there are very many positions in which an octagonal building shows but three sides to the eye, and the impulse to double the number seen for the whole number of sides is very natural.

The stockade has all been removed except the old sally port already spoken of, which does duty as part of the wall of a wagon shed ; but twenty years ago when the present owner, Mr. Call, first went to Ross, the stockade was complete. It was built of three-inch redwood planks set upright in a slot in solid logs imbedded in the ground, was twelve or fourteen feet high, and surmounted by a cheval de frise of iron spikes. Loopholes for musketry and embrasures for cannon were in proper places, especially around the portal. The stockade was one hundred varas, 275 feet, square, according to Vallejo ; 300 x 280 feet according to another authority, 1088 feet in circumference by the inventory of sale to Sutter.

The chapel is in better preservation than the bastions, though it makes one's heart ache to see how it needs a little care that would do much toward preserving it ; just a nail here and there, where a loose plank will be ripped off the roof by the next gale for the lack of it. The building on the exterior still bears quite a churchlike look, with its square belfry and curious round cupola ; the roof on the weather side is nearly bare, but under the lee of the cupola has gathered a sod some three inches thick, which bears a fine crop of foxtail grass. In the interior the sacrilegious hand has wrought havoc, for the building has been used as a stable and is fitted up with stalls. The modern Californian cares more for his horses than for his soul.

Still there can be made out with study the early arrangement of the edifice. The round cupola is nearly over where the altar must have been, and is open over it, while the rest of the room is ceiled. We climbed up the narrow steps to the ghostly attic and up into the belfry, noting everywhere the great solid beams and fine joinery in this hand-hewn timbering and planking that is characteristic of all the Russian work at Ross.

It is said that in its prime there were fine paintings in this chapel,—eikons like the famous Sitka Madonna. Nothing of this kind is left, but there is an old hand-carved lectern and great candlestick that show much patience and skill in cutting out the round forms now so easy to make with a lathe. In the bar-room of the hotel establishment are two quaint old pews or seats from the chapel. They are rudely made of solid three-inch sticks, and the seat is so deep that one thinks that there must have been giants in those days to have such amazing length of thigh. Possibly furs or upholstering, now all gone, may have filled in some of the space.

The old cemetery is another interesting spot. It lies across the gulch to the eastward of the Fort, on the brow of a hill where the ocean breeze sways the arm of the wooden cross as it hangs rusted loose on its wrought-iron nail. There are signs of a dozen or more graves beside the curious wooden structure shown in the sketch (p. 8) and the round wooden pillar. This pillar is said to have had a carved top and cross above it, now gone. Some of the Fort people speak of it as the whipping post, but I can hardly believe that that useful appliance could have been so far away from the Fort. It is a matter of record that there was whipping enough, as well as many executions, in the stern discipline of the Fort.

The graves are marked by wooden slabs prone on the earth. These slabs seem to have had no inscription on them as a rule. One with an inscription was found a few years ago and brought to San Francisco, but so many of the letters were gone that it proved undecipherable. The letters had been painted on, and the paint had preserved the wood under it so that they seemed to be carved. It was probably only an ordinary record of name and dates. It was given to the Woodward collection, and perhaps lost in the recent dispersion of that property.

A few years ago Mrs. Gertrude Atherton, who made Fort Ross a hermitage for literary work, bribed some of the boys at the hotel to go over with her and excavate one of these graves. The redwood coffin was found in good preservation, except that the lid had fallen in and the interior was filled with earth. Search in this showed the shin bones, the soles of the shoes, and some buttons, all that remained to indicate that there had been an occupant. Mrs. Atherton was much disgusted; for she needed a dead Russian for literary purposes, and had hoped at least to get an officer with his trappings, if not indeed records buried with him.

There are now not so many buildings at Ross as in Russian days: hardly more than a score are left of the fifty-nine tha are spoken of as being there at one time. There is truth in the remark of the landlord: "Guess it was livelier times here eighty years ago." The present population is but fifty souls. There is a post office and a store, as well as the schoolhouse, hotel, and saloon mentioned. The school is taught by Miss Call, daughter of the owner of the Fort, and consists of nine children, —three of one family and six of another. Some fifty small schooners a year are loaded at the little landing with wood, fence posts, tan bark, and dairy products.

But business was calling us back to the city, in spite of the dreamy charm of this romantic old spot, and so we prepared to "go down below," as they speak of it there,—an expression that gained color from our unwillingness to return to the world,—and the rest of them.

One of the landlords took us up the grade again, and beguiled the way with pleasing converse. He told us the supplement to the stage driver's narrative of how the stage was robbed.

"A young fellow came along, kind o' slick looking, and asked if he might stop awhile. Then he wanted to jim around a little to pay for his board, and we set him to fixin' things up about the place. Soon we found out that he was pretty bad medicine, and I told him that he had better move on. He had found out where everything lay, and that night he and another fellow came back, and bored around the lock of the saloon building door, and stole a rifle and a shotgun, and some cigars and liquor. The next day they held up the stage at the Bend of the Cañon. They caught them afterward, and they are now in San Quentin."

Soon the stage came along and we got in, to insult with our freshness the feelings of one weary passenger, who had been riding since six o'clock the evening before, without a wink of sleep all night. A day in the "wet dust" of the road and the rush of the train, and we were through with our trip.

The importance of the episode that Fort Ross stands for lies here, in my mind. The Northern world has been brought under European civilization by two currents; one moving west, the one sung by good Bishop Berkeley, familiar to us all—not perfect, indeed, but on the whole making for freedom and light, and working itself clearer as time goes on,—and the other moving east, though the whole width of Asia, the Aleutian chain, and down the west coast of America. This current has been little celebrated in song and story, for, sadly mingled with Asiatic barbarism, its mark is absolutism and cruelty. Ross, and Bodega, its appendage, are the extreme westerly mark of this current. There it met and was turned backward by the westward stream of empire, which has now made the whole of America free. No man can prophesy that the end is yet.

THE RUSSIAN COLONIES IN AMERICA
1897

In 1897 Arthur Inkersley published a very
interesting article devoted to the Russian
colonies in America before the Alaskan purchase. The article sheds light on the early history of the Russian colonies, and
their development under Alexander Baranov,
a capable manager of the Russian-American
Company, who was the dominant figure of Russian Alaska during the first three decades
of the nineteenth century.

Source: <u>Overland Monthly</u>, vol. XXX, section
2 (July 1897), pp. 9-22.

N DECEMBER 8, 1741, in a
wretched little hut on the
island off the coast of Kamchatka, which still bears his
name, the intrepid explorer,
Vitus Bering, died. Though
a Dane by birth, he had been
for many years in the service
of the Tsar, and it was on his voyages and
those of his able lieutenant, Chirikof, that
the Russians mainly based their claim to
territory in northwestern America.

From this time forth Russian traders and
merchants made frequent expeditions to
America in quest of valuable furs, but they
behaved so brutally that even now, at the
distance of a century and a half, the memory
of their cruelties has not been blotted from
the minds of the natives. Very various
fortunes attended the trading and exploring
expeditions of those days; some vessels
brought back large quantities of splendid
furs, while the crews of others suffered
terrible hardships and realized nothing in
return.

After Kadiak and the islands of the Aleutian group had been visited, the imperial
government thought it time to take steps
for the more accurate mapping out of the
regions discovered by the Siberian traders.
Accordingly several naval officers were detailed, on double pay and with increased
rank, to accompany the traders, take notes
of the resources and productions the country,
and make astronomical observations. But the

demon of ill-luck seemed to pursue these
specially chosen officers, for though they
made gallant efforts to extend their knowledge, and incurred serious dangers, they
added very little to the information already
acquired by the traders.

At this period most of the trading and
exploration was done by companies organized for these purposes. The expeditions
extended over three, four, five, or more
years. On their return the total results
were divided into two parts; the projectors
of the expedition took one, and the other
was divided into shares, of which each
sailor and participator received one or two.
Many of these exploring parties met with
disaster at sea, but these were almost wholly
due to utter ignorance of the simplest principles of navigation on the part of the
adventurers, who were traders, hunters, and
trappers, but not sailors.

When the game on the Aleutian islands
and the adjoining peninsula began to become
scarce, it was decided to try to make fresh
discoveries on the mainland. The first
attempts were not successful, the natives
offering a brave resistance and repulsing the
Russians with considerable loss. In 1783 a
company of Siberian merchants organized an
expedition on a larger scale than any that
had hitherto left the shores of Siberia: it
consisted of three ships and numbered
nearly two hundred men. One of the vessels
was called The Three Saints, and was commanded by Grigor Ivanovich Shelikof, who,

with his crew, wintered on Bering island, and then passed on to Copper and other islands. A somewhat long stay was made at Unalashka, where they took on fresh water, supplies, and several Aleutian hunters. Thence they sailed to the island now called Kadiak, and anchored in Three Saints harbor. Here they were received with hostility by the natives, but, nothing daunted, they began to build houses and to erect fortifications for a permanent settlement. The winter was spent at Karluk, where salmon were very plentiful, and where at the present day several canneries are situated.

Shelikof now became very anxious to secure a monopoly of the Russian discoveries and settlements in North America, and to obtain for his company the exclusive privilege of trading in the new colonies. To further his plans, he went back to Siberia, leaving in command of the colonies a Siberian merchant named Samoilof, to whom he gave instructions which give us a high idea of his wisdom and clear-sightedness. Shelikof directed his lieutenant to extend the sphere of Russian influence to the eastward and southward, to keep out foreign traders, to establish stations further and further along the coast of the American continent, and to set up marks of Russian occupation as far south as California. Samoilof was also instructed to send natives to Siberia to study the language, domestic life, and customs, of the Russians, so that on returning to their tribes they might aid in civilizing their countrymen; to collect ores, minerals, and shells, gather articles of native manufacture, make surveys, build block-houses, and establish schools.

Shelikof journeyed on to Irkutsk, the capital of Eastern Siberia, where he placed before the Governor-General, for transmission to Saint Petersburg, a long account of his discoveries, accompanied by maps and plans, and asked recognition of his work. The Governor-General took the matter up with enthusiasm, and fortunately for the success of Shelikof's schemes, the Russian government just about this time became convinced that many abuses existed in the relations between the various independent trading companies and the natives, and that it would be best to abolish the traders' rule, and place the whole American traffic in the hands of a single strong company. So Shelikof and his partner, Golikof, were invited to Saint Petersburg to be presented to the Empress, who manifested great interest in their projects, and conferred gold medals and swords of honor upon them. On September 28th, 1788, a decree was issued, giving the company exclusive privileges of trading and hunting in the regions discovered and controlled by them. Besides all this a subsidy of two hundred thousand rubles was advanced from the public treasury, to be repaid in twenty annual instalments without interest.

In Siberia Shelikof looked about him for a man who would carry out his plans, and set his heart upon Alexander Baranof, a native of Kargapol in eastern Russia. Baranof was born in 1747, and from his native place went to Moscow, where he was a clerk in retail shops; in 1771 he set up in business for himself, but dissatisfied with his prospects, he migrated to Siberia in 1780, and took the management of a glass factory in Irkutsk. Later, he engaged in trading on the Anadir river and in Kamchatka, and did a fair business. Being fond of his independence, he at first refused to enter the service of the Shelikof company. So Delarof, a Greek, was appointed in charge of the colony at Kadiak. He behaved with great kindness and justice; but, though visitors of all nationalities praised him highly, he was much too lenient and honest to suit his unscrupulous directors.

In 1789 Baranof lost two of his caravans, and was rendered bankrupt. Shelikof approached him again, and this time Baranof accepted his overtures, and entered the service of the company in 1790. He was excellently fitted for the work he had to do; shrewd, politic, full of courage and energy, careful to avoid disputes, and yet not burdened with inconvenient scruples. That he was fond of strong liquor, loose in his relationships with women, and capable of lying whenever occasion seemed to require, did not detract from, but rather increased his usefulness in the post he was called to occupy.

Baranof sailed to the scene of his future labors in The Three Saints, but he was not destined to reach Kadiak that year. The ship was wrecked on Unalashka and went to pieces. Baranof at once showed his readiness of resource by distributing his fifty-two men over the island in search of seals and edible roots, and his energy by helping them to build underground huts in which to pass the long and cold winter. Though food often ran short, and many hardships had to be endured, Baranof learned much about the habits and customs of the natives that afterwards proved useful to him.

In the spring of 1791 the Russians constructed three bidarkas, or skin boats, in which they safely reached Kadiak, making many valuable explorations on the way. Delarof was relieved, and Baranof assumed command of all the forts, stations, and settlements, of the Shelikof-Golikof company, the principal post being at the bay of Three Saints, Kadiak. But his domain did not extend much beyond Kadiak and a few of the adjacent islands, as several private trading companies were yet in operation on the Aleutian islands and Prince William sound. After Baranof had been in power for some little time, he determined to extend the company's sphere of influence, and to seize the Alexander archipelago.

With these ends in view, Baranof removed the chief settlement of the company from Three Saints to Saint Paul harbor, because more timber for ship-building could be obtained near the latter place. He made an alliance with the chief of a tribe of natives, and while on an exploring expedition met with an English ship, the captain of which gave him a good deal of useful information. He effected a landing upon Nuchek island, but was attacked by a large body of natives, wearing wooden armor and carrying wooden shields strong enough to stop a bullet, and using arrows tipped with flint or copper. The natives fought stubbornly and the fortune of the day was turning against the Russians when some Aleuts in their service escaped to a Russian vessel anchored not far from the battle-field, and brought aid to Baranof. At last the natives were defeated and driven off, partly by the aid of a one-and-a-half-pounder gun of the Russians. Baranof wrote of this battle to Shelikof as follows:—

As for myself, God protected me; though my shirt was torn by a spear and the arrows fell thickly around me. Being aroused from a deep sleep, I had no time to dress, but rushed out as I was to encourage the men and to see that our only cannon was moved to wherever the danger was greatest. Great praise is due to the fearless demeanor of my men, many of whom were new recruits.

Baranof had intended to spend the winter on Prince William sound, but the hostility of the natives induced him to return to Kadiak. Here he received instructions from his directors to begin shipbuilding at once, with the aid of an English ship-builder sent to him from Siberia. But as winter quarters for his men were more pressingly needed than ships, he set to work to construct them first. There being no suitable timber for shipbuilding on Kadiak or Afognak islands, he erected quarters for his ship-carpenters on the shores of Sunday bay in Prince William sound, and all through the winter the work of felling trees went on. But tar and oakum for calking were entirely lacking, and the necessary iron had to be collected from the wrecks of vessels. Some iron ore was found, and Baranof made many attempts to smelt iron, but he was unsuccessful. Besides all this, food was scarce; and had Baranof not been possessed of indomitable energy and perseverance, the work could never have been accomplished. An last he triumphed over all difficulties, and the first ship built in northwestern America was launched. She was named the Phœnix and must have been an odd-looking craft. She was seventy-three feet long on the water-line, and seventy-nine feet over all, with a depth of thirteen and one half feet and a beam of twenty-three feet. She was built of spruce timber, and her capacity was about one hundred tons. The sails were made of scraps of canvas raked together from the company's warehouses in Kamchatka and the colonies, and presented a motley appearance. For paint a mixture of tar and whale-oil was used, and as there was not enough even of this to cover the whole vessel, the rest was coated with spruce gum and oil. With great difficulty she made her way to Kadiak, where her appearance was hailed with joy. Being refitted, she made a quick passage to Okhotsk in Siberia, where she was supplied with cabins, deckhouses, and new sails and rigging. The Shelikof company was very proud of their own vessel, built in their own yard, and henceforth she made regular trips between Okhotsk and the American colonies. In 1795 Baranof built and launched two more vessels, the Dolphin and the Olga.

It has been said that the Shelikof company was not the only trading company doing business in Russian America. About five years before Baranof took charge of affairs at Kadiak the Lebedef company had sent a vessel with thirty-eight men thither, but the agents of the Shelikof company, not wishing to have their hunting-grounds encroached upon, recommended them to go on to Cook's Inlet, where they established a permanent settlement, named Saint George, consisting of log buildings surrounded by a stockade. The Shelikof company already had a fort, named Saint Alexander, at the entrance of the inlet. It was square, with bastions at two of the corners, and had a gate protected by two guns. Inside were dwellings and warehouses, on one of which was a lookout tower. In 1791 the Lebedef company's ship, Saint George, reached the inlet. The commander beached his ship and began to erect a stockaded fort, to which the name of Saint Nicholas was given.

At these fortified posts the Russians took things pretty easily, making the natives go out hunting for them, and themselves doing little more than guard-duty. The domestic work was performed by the female hostages, helped by the children who had been sent by native chiefs to learn Russian manners and customs at the post. Now and then the band would set out on a marauding expedition, in the course of which they plundered their own countrymen and the natives with a cheerful lack of discrimination. The Lebedef men at Fort Saint Nicholas soon became a nuisance and a terror to the whole country, robbing the natives of their furs without payment, pillaging the stores of their own countrymen, and carrying off their native servants and hostages.

At last the news of their outrages and quarrels reached Baranof, who, though angry, was restrained from taking immediate measures by the fact that Shelikof was a partner in the Lebedef company, and Baranof did not wish to interfere without communicating with his chief. So he contented himself for the present with warning the men at Fort Saint Nicholas that he would not permit any outrages likely to injure trade. In spite of this, quarrels occurred continually, and attacks and ambuscades were almost daily events. Towards the end of 1793 Baranof received reinforcements which made up the total number of his men to about one hundred and fifty. The Lebedef men were not much fewer in number, were superior to Baranof's men in dash and

recklessness, and occupied an excellent position with easy access to supplies. At last Baranof's shipyard at Sunday harbor was in danger, and this roused him to vigorous action. He summoned the commander of Saint Nicholas to his presence, and put him in irons, but he failed to do much to restrain the excesses of the rival traders.

Soon, however, Baranof's hands were much strengthened by his receiving authority to form settlements anywhere in America, and to control the country for five hundred versts round them. Against such extensive powers the other trading companies could do nothing, and ere long they abandoned their posts, leaving the Shelikof company master of the field. But their crimes and outrages had seriously injured trade by arousing the animosity of the natives against the Russians. Baranof, therefore, made great efforts to reassure the natives and to maintain order among his subordinates. He patched up, to the best of his ability, the discontent existing among the company's employees, and told them that he would redress their grievances. By firmness and an autocratic demeanor he rapidly gained great ascendency over them.

The Shelikof company, anxious to undertake fresh enterprises, requested the imperial authorities to send out to the colonies Siberian exiles skilled in ironwork, blacksmithing, and agriculture. In August, 1794, in response to this request, two of the Shelikof company's vessels arrived at Saint Paul with a cargo of stores, cattle, and provisions, and carrying 192 persons, of whom fifty-two were craftsmen and agriculturists. Baranof was instructed to use his taste and judgment in selecting a site on the mainland for a Russian settlement, which he was to make as trim and neat as possible, not permitting the Russians to live in such squalor and untidiness as did many of their countrymen in Siberia. The settlement was to have spacious squares and wide streets radiating from them. The streets were to be bordered with trees, and the houses built with spaces intervening, so that they might spread over a larger area and give a more imposing appearance to the town.

Nor was Shelikof content with all this. He was busy building ships for a company which then held the Pribylof islands, organizing the North American company, and extending traffic from Unalashka to the Arctic ocean. He established a central office at Irkutsk for the control of his many American enterprises, thus paving the way for the future consolidation of all the Russian companies in America.

Much had already been done in America. the best localities for raising cattle and for agriculture had been chosen and fortified : hunting grounds and sites for harbors and trading-posts had been selected. The colonists had been pretty successful in raising vegetables, and in some places even cereals, and plenty of excellent fish was always obtainable. By magnifying his conquests and representing that he had added fifty thousand subjects to the Russian empire, Shelikof produced so good an impression on the imperial authorities that he gained for his company the exclusive privilege of trading throughout Russian America, and on the islands between it and Asia. Shelikof's daughter had married Rezanof, a man of good family and great influence. Rezanof formed the ambitious project of procuring from the Empress a charter as wide as that of the British East India company, and of adding an empire as vast as India to the realms of the Tsar. His far-reaching schemes received a check by the death in 1795 at Irkutsk of Shelikof, who must be regarded as the founder of the Russian colonies in America ; and by the death in 1796 of the Empress, before she had granted the extensive charter he hoped for.

However, Natalia, Shelikof's widow, undertook the management of the company, and being a woman of great energy and intelligence, though of little education, with the aid of her son-in-law, she conducted its affairs with much shrewdness and discretion. In 1798 the imperial government, thinking that by giving exclusive privilege to one strong company the natives would be protected, disorder prevented, the fur-bearing animals saved from extermination, and Russian authority firmly established in America, permitted an association with three quarters of a million rubles (about $577,000) capital, and known as the United American comany, to be formed. It had been feared that the death of the Empress would be fatal to the schemes of the association, but Rezanof, by constant attendance on her successor, Paul I, obtained confirmation of the act of consolidation of the United American com-

pany, to which the name of the Russian American company was given.

The company was granted the exclusive privilege for twenty years of hunting, fishing, exploring, trading, founding, and building settlements on the northwestern mainland of America and the islands from Kamchatka west to the coast of America, and south to the shores of Japan. No rivals, even though having posts already established within these limits, if not united with the Russian American company, were permitted to do any of these things. The civil and military authorities stationed at these places were ordered to give help and protection to the officers of the company. In return for these large and exclusive privileges the company bound itself to maintain a mission of the Græco-Catholic church, the members of which were to accompany all trading, hunting, and exploring expeditions, where an opportunity for Christianizing natives might occur. The company also undertook to encourage agriculture, cattle-breeding, ship-building, and other industries among the Russian settlers in America, and to maintain friendly relations with the natives.

The news of the organization of the Russian American company reached Baranof at a time when things were looking very black for him. He was suffering from ill health, his men were short of provisions, one of his sloops had recently been wrecked, and parties of his hunters attacked and killed by the Thlinket Indians. His drooping courage was revived, and amid many dangers and hardships, he made his way to Norfolk, or Sitka sound, and landed at a place called still Old Sitka, about three miles to the north of the present town. A Sitkan chief coming up to ask his purpose, Baranof replied that the Emperor of Russia wished to establish a settlement for trade there. The chief gave him a small piece of ground, on which Baranof erected a strong two-story building, guarded by a palisade and two blockhouses, and named Fort Archangel Gabriel. In the autumn of 1800, Baranof, having fairly started the Sitka settlement, returned to Kadiak.

Matters did not long remain quiet at Sitka after Baranof's departure. The natives were supplied with guns, ammunition, and spirits, by English and American vessels trading with them, and soon became bold enough to form the plan of attacking and destroying the Russian settlement. To this end they secured allies from the Alexander archipelago and the Stikine River district. In June, 1802, the barracks and fort were attacked by large numbers of natives, while most of the garrison were out hunting. The commander and many of his men were killed; the cattle-sheds and warehouses were taken and set on fire, and also the ships lying at anchor off the settlement. Three Russians and five Aleuts managed to escape to an English ship, whose captain made the Sitkan chiefs drunk, and recovered a large quantity of the valuable sea-otter skins which the natives had pillaged from the post. With these he sailed to Kadiak, where he received ten thousand rubles (nearly eight thousand dollars) as salvage.

In 1803 Baranof received the news of his appointment as a shareholder in the company, and of permission to wear the gold medal of the Order of Saint Vladimir. But gratified as he was at these marks of imperial approval, he was burning with anxiety to recover Sitka. With this purpose he directed his lieutenant at Yakutat (where the company had a block-house and stockade for the Siberian agriculturists in their service) to build two sailing-vessels. In 1804 he started out with an expeditionary force, consisting of eight hundred Aleuts in three hundred bidarkas, and one hundred and twenty Russians on board four small vessels under the command of a lieutenant; Baranof himself commanding the sloops Ekaterina and Alexander.

Soon after Baranof had left Kadiak, a ship named the Neva came out from Kronstadt to Kadiak. Not finding Baranof there, her commander, Lisiansky, sailed after him to Sitka, where his aid proved very welcome. The Sitka natives had taken up a strong position on a bluff, called Katlean's rock, or the Kekoor, at the mouth of Indian river. Here they occupied a fort built of logs and protected by a breastwork two logs thick.

The Russians landed and attempted to take the stockade by assault, but the natives made a brave resistance, keeping up so good a fire that they killed or wounded twenty-six Russians, among whom was Baranof himself. Next day Lisiansky assumed the command, and attacked the natives so vigorously that they offered to make peace, and promised to give hostages and to evacuate the fort. But as they showed no signs of giving up the stronghold, guns were brought up on a raft and trained upon the fort. The natives endured the strange and unwonted sounds of the bombardment during the day, but at night, after killing their dogs and strangling their infant children, that no sound might show their purpose, they secretly abandoned the post, which the captors burned.

The Russians then set to work to provide permanent quarters for themselves; they constructed three substantial buildings with a stockade having block-houses at each corner; kitchen-gardens were planted and cattle introduced. The name of New Archangel was given to the settlement. Part of the stockade separating the Russian quarters from the Indian rancherie remained until a recent date. The natives entered into a treaty with the Russians and were presented with cloaks and medals. In the autumn of 1806 Baranof returned from New Archangel to Saint Paul, leaving Kuskof in command, with orders to build ships and to finish certain structures already begun.

During the year 1803 (the year after the capture of Sitka by the natives) Baranof, ever desirous to extend the operations of the company, was pushing forward in the direction of the Spanish colonies, and especially of California. Baranof lent to an American captain named O'Cain twenty bidarkas and several hunters in charge of Shutzof, an employee of the company. Shutzof was instructed to take careful observations of the inhabitants of the coast of California, and to look out for new hunting-grounds. The American vessel left Kadiak at the end of October, 1803, sailed down to San Diego, and thence to the Bay of San Quintin in Lower California, where about a thousand skins were secured. The results of this expedition were so satisfactory that Baranof was induced in 1808 to furnish Captain Ayres, of the ship Mercury from Boston, with twenty-five bidarkas, to hunt in islands not known before. The ship was to be out ten or twelve months, and on her return the proceeds were to be equally divided. On the way south sea-otter and beaver skins were procured by barter from the natives of the

Charlotte islands and at the mouth of the Columbia river. Thence the ship proceeded to San Francisco and San Diego, and came back with more than two thousand skins.

Between 1806 and 1812 Baranof entered into several similar contracts with American captains. In 1808 he sent two vessels to the coast of New Albion, a land of vague extent, the southern limit of which was somewhere between Point Reyes and San Diego. One of these was wrecked at the mouth of Quay harbor, and the other, commanded by Kuskof, returned after an absence of about a year with more than two thousand otter skins, and the information that the coast had many localities suitable for agriculture and ship-building, and that the whole country to the north of San Francisco was unoccupied by any European power. Accordingly, Baranof gathered men suitable for an agricultural settlement, skilled in raising stock and tilling fields, and sent them in 1810 to New Albion with orders to make further explorations. On the way the crew was attacked by the Queen Charlotte islanders, and returned to New Archangel. Next year they started out again, and on this voyage Kuskof selected a spot eighteen miles north of Bodega bay, where he bought some land from the natives. In 1812 the colony was founded and named Ross. But as a place for agriculture and ship-building it was a failure, and the hunting-grounds near it were soon exhausted. The story of Fort Ross has been fully told by Mr. Charles S. Greene in the OVERLAND for July, 1893.

Quiet and dull as Sitka now looks under the government of the United States, it was in Baranof's day a very busy place. Bricks for the huge fireplaces in the Russian houses were made there: boats and sailing-vessels were built in a well-equipped shipyard: there were wood-turneries and woolen manufactories; and agricultural implements from the foundries were sold all down the Pacific Coast as far as Mexico. Axes and knives were made for bartering with the natives at the trading posts, and almost all the Mission churches from the north of Alaska to Mexico were supplied with bells from the brass-foundries of Sitka. From six hundred to eight hundred whites lived in the town in those days; and more than a dozen sailing vessels were constantly employed in trading.

In 1809 a serious plot was formed by some Siberian ex-convicts against Baranof, but it was betrayed to him and promptly crushed. Baranof had for some time been growing anxious to be relieved from his onerous labors as Chief Manager, and the discovery of this plot increased his desire. He repeatedly requested the directors of the company to appoint a successor, but twice the man selected to relieve him died before reaching his post.

In 1815 the imperial government, in conjunction with the Russian American company, sent out two vessels, the Kutuzof and the Suvarof, under command of Hagemeister, who was authorized to assume control of the affairs of the company in place of Baranof, if upon investigation he thought it necessary to do so. Hagemeister did not inform Baranof of the extent of his powers, but quietly examined the condition of the company. Baranof was still working earnestly in its service, but the intrepid pioneer's fierce energy was beginning to flicker out. He had always been careless of religion, but now he suddenly conceived a liking for the church, and constantly kept a priest near him. Yanovsky, the first lieutenant of the Suvarof, fell in love with Baranof's daughter, and obtained her father's consent to their marriage. But Hagemeister's consent was also necessary, and was only granted on the condition that Lieutenant Yanovsky should stay for two years at New Archangel, and act as representative of the Chief Manager.

On January 11, 1818, Hagemeister told Baranof of his instructions, which so surprised and prostrated the old man that he never quite recovered from the shock. But it was the work of months to render full accounts, and to turn the affairs of the company over to the company's commissioner, Klebnikof. The commissioner estimated the value of the property at New Archangel, to say nothing of that at the many other stations of the company, at two and one half millions of rubles; and besides this, the Suvarof took furs to the value of two hundred thousand rubles to Europe, and left behind in the storehouses furs worth nine hundred thousand rubles more. The buildings and vessels of the company were in excellent condition, and the accounts in perfect order. In September, 1818, the work was done and the complete statement handed over to Yanovsky. It was now nearly thirty years since Baranof had landed on Kadiak island; he was already seventy-two years old, and had spent himself in the service of the company. Thrown unceremoniously aside in his old age by the company whose leading spirit he had been, and whose interests he had enormously extended and firmly consolidated, he could not tear himself away at once from the scenes of his labors, dangers, privations, and achievements. He resolved to pay farewell visits to Kadiak and the various settlements he had founded, and then go to live with a brother in Kamchatka. But he was urged to return to Russia, where his advice would be of the highest value to the directors of the company. He decided to do this, and late in November set sail in the Kutusof, which, on her way home, stopped for more than a month at the unhealthy port of Batavia. Here Baranof insisted upon going ashore. He was seized with sickness, and died soon after the vessel had set sail again.

Like Napoleon, Baranof was a little great man; insignificant in appearance, thin, short of stature, with reddish hair, and a face covered by hardship and exposure with wrinkles. He was an early riser, and ate but one meal a day, and that at no fixed time. He was fond of gayety, and kept round him a little court of reckless spirits, whom he feasted and filled with strong liquors. Ship-captains who did not drink stood but small chance of doing business with him. Washington Irving, in his "Astoria," describes, with a few touches of exaggeration, but on the whole faithfully, how the ship-masters who visited New Archangel sang and reveled with the Chief Manager. He was fitful and violent in temper, but always showed such sincere regret and desire to make amends for outbursts of passion that the women and servants of his house came to look upon them as the precursors of a feast. He was fond of music, and his daughter, to whom he was much attached, could always put him into a good humor by playing on the piano. He treated his daughter with much respect, and used to send her away from the room when he began to feel drunk. One day, finding her German governess drinking a glass of spirits, he struck her; next day he expressed regret for his act, but said that she must never let his daughter see her drinking strong liquor.

Yet rough as Baranof was, he was kind to people in distress, and generous to his employees. Though he had boundless chances of self-enrichment, he did not avail himself of them. He spent liberally but did not exceed his means. He maintained his wife well at his native place, Kargapol, and made many remittances to Russia to help the families of men who had died in the company's service; he also gave part of his shares in the company to supplement the scanty incomes of his lieutenants, Banner and Kuskof. The company's commissioner, Klebnikof, who was thoroughly familiar with the details of Baranof's management, entertained the liveliest admiration for him. He wrote a biography of Baranof, which is really, as it could not well help being, a history of the Russian colonies in America.

It may be well to say a few words about the finances of the company of which Baranof, if not the founder, was at least the controlling spirit. The original capital of the company was about $542,000, afterwards increased to about $925,000. The net earnings between 1797 and 1820 were about $5,764,000, of which rather more than half was paid out in dividends, the remainder being added to the capital. Furs to the value of twelve millions of dollars were sold or exchanged for commodities at Kiakhta, and for more than $2,600,000 at Canton. Yet the yield of furs was by no means so great during the later as in the earlier years of Baranof's administration, the sea-otters falling off very much in numbers, and the competition of American traders, who had no scruples about giving guns and ammunition in barter to the natives, doing the company much harm. The Chief Manager received $5,800 per annum, the chief clerk from $2,250 to $3,000, a priest $450, and a hunter from $45 to $112. Provisions had to be purchased at the company's stores, and were often scarce and dear, owing to the failure of ships to arrive. The company's employees frequently had to put up with serious hardships, and had but little chance of laying up anything for their old age.

Many traces of Baranof and his successors are still visible at Sitka. Near the water's edge, and overlooking the lovely bay, is Katlean's rock. On this eminence of about eighty feet Baranof built a block-house, which was burned. A later Chief Manager, Kupreanof, crowned the rock with a spacious residence, which was destroyed by earthquake in 1847. The next structure, generally called the Castle, measured eighty-six by fifty-one feet, and was built of squared cedar logs, riveted by copper bolts to their rocky foundation. It had three stories and was surmounted by a light-house. It was handsomely furnished, and there the naval officers who succeeded Baranof lived luxuriously, entertaining visitors of all ranks with a lavish and impartial hospitality. When the "Castle" was turned over to the United States by Prince Demitrius Maksontoff, the only military governor, it was in thorough order, but the American soldiers stripped it of all its furniture and decorations, and it rapidly became ruinous and forlorn. On the arrival of a man-of-war or a revenue cutter some of the large rooms would be furnished up for a dance, after which desolation again reigned. A year or two ago it perished by fire.

The Custom House, the barracks occupied by the United States marines, and some stout log-built warehouses near the wharf also owe their origin to the Russians. If we cross the grassy parade-ground, where once was the Russian ship-yard, and walk towards the Greek church, we pass on the right a sturdy log structure which was the main office of the Russian American company. Behind the church is a building formerly used as a club-house by the Russian officers. Not far from the club were tea-gardens and a race-course, both now entirely hidden under the mantle of dense vegetation that rapidly covers every deserted spot in the moist climate of southeastern Alaska. The saw-mill with the flume that supplied it with water is still visible, though rapidly falling into decay. Another legacy of the Muscovite to the American is the walk leading round the curving beach to the woods bordering the banks of Indian river. This charming promenade furnishes the residents of Sitka with the chance of obtaining a little pedestrian exercise, a great boon in a country where there are practically no roads.

RUSSIAN OLD BELIEVERS IN PITTSBURGH
1914

After several decades of Russian immigration to the United States, among the newly
arrived settlers were important segments
of Russian Old Believers who left their
native country because of religious persecutions. Many of them established themselves in the Pittsburgh, Pennsylvania,
area. After visiting a community of Russian Old Believers, A. Sokoloff described
their life in an article from which we have
extracted relevant portions.

Source: Survey, vol. 33 (November 7, 1914),
pp. 145-151.

I was soon punished for my fa-
tuity, however, by another snap-
shot view. I had come with special
purpose to make acquaintance with
the Old Believers in Cokeburgh, a
mining town to all purposes exactly like
many others of the Pittsburgh district,
but containing an especially large number of Russians. Out of between 400
or 500 miners (almost all foreigners)
300 were my countrymen, about half of
them Old Believers.

I reached Cokeburgh on a beautiful
early Sunday morning. I was disagree-
ably struck, on leaving the train, with
the sound of what seemed to be drunken
brawls sounding from many houses.
Such indeed they were. Yesterday had
been pay-day, and bearded men were
drinking and drunk. Many houses were
deserted, the revelers being grouped in
a few. An ugly sight! Dirty, dishev-
eled men in filthy kitchens filled with
empty bottles, kegs and barrels; everything helter-skelter. Worst of all was
the foul language they were using, without any provocation, regardless of the
presence of children. I knew they did
not use those bad words in the north of
Russia. This is the influence of sol-
diery, so numerous in Poland and on
the borderline and so hateful everywhere. But when I rebuked them, in

quiet unrestrained expressions, for their
foul language, nobody knocked me
down; they were ashamed, for a while
at least. They felt insulted only when
I refused to drink a glass of beer with
them, invariably offered without prelim-
inaries. Many were sitting in the room
with their hats on—a thing I would not
have believed about a Russian peasant.

The women were by themselves elsewhere, untidy, some barefooted, and almost all in weekday clothes. "Why is
this so here," I asked myself, "when I
remember the streets of Russian villages
on Sunday, bright with all the colors of
the rainbow in the women's bands,
frocks and kerchiefs?" Possibly the
answer was to be found in the fact that
the nearest church of Old Believers
was about forty miles from Cokeburgh,
and Russian Sunday adornment is in-
separable from church-going. Only
girls of marriageable age, or close to it,
were displaying quite American apparel
and hairdressing, and this without any
connection with the length of time they
had lived in America. A nice American
lady to whom I showed the picture on
the preceding page, when she saw the
girl standing first from the left said that
she must have been in this country most
of her life. Yet she had been here only
six months. I talked with her and found

her fresh, with rustic, awkward bash-fulness. .

The village "belle" was also a daughter of the Old Believers, but she had been brought up in this country.. Refined in feature and of slender figure, she spoke perfect English, yet showed much of that defiant, overbearing lack of kindness one meets so often in the city shop-girl, whose manners she was evidently imitating. I wished her to pose for a picture with her uncle, but she balked at the suggestion of being photographed with such an un-American object. She could not see, as I did, what a majestic head of a boyar her uncle had,—so much like Boyar Morosoff, he who refused to sit "below" a man beneath him in rank at the Czar's table, and being ordered to don a buffon's dress so taunted the Czar with bitter truth and insults that he was beheaded for dessert.

The large woman in the middle of the group was possessor of the sole abstinent husband among the Old Believers, a small taciturn man. "They do not like him; they don't like anybody who does not drink with them," explained the woman, "so he stays at home." He proved to have been in America about seventeen years (the longest term in America of any Russian that I met) and six years in Cokeburgh. Nothing in his manner or in the appearance of his house, though it was decent enough (his wife and he had no children, no boarders), showed particularly the influence of America. There was neither the quaintness of the Russian "izba" about their barren room, nor the comfort and neatness of the American home.

Later, in another mining town in the north of Allegheny County—Russeltown, called by Russians, "Wet Mines"—I vainly tried to find shelter for the night in some Old Believer's house. My companion was a Russian, just beginning in the business of bookselling. Three men at that time were making their livings by selling books, holy images, and crosses, but mainly books, among Russians in and around Pittsburgh. Ready enough were the Old Believers to let us into their houses, but these were crowded beyond belief. The rumor that Wet Mines was about to start up had brought a multitude from other places.

"Say, Beard, do you have a room in your house for tonight?" This to a burly fellow hardly distinguishable for the darkness, yet unmistakably an Old Believer. "But, my 'bratets' (my dear little brother)," he kindly responded (I was ashamed at having apostrophized him so roughly), "I have just moved to the town and have no furniture whatever in my house; it's on the way. If you don't care—welcome." And this welcome comes out of the darkness to a stranger of whom the "Beard" can see only that he is from the city (a bad recommendation indeed) and that he can talk Russian. No asking to which of the sixty-six nationalities in Russia and almost as many religions he belonged, but straight out, "Welcome." True, there was not very much to which the visitors were welcomed—a quite empty house, a bundle of shawls spread upon a pile of straw in one room—all the furnishings they possessed—and nothing at all in the other. An attractive-looking woman was sitting on the floor gazing dreamily into the blazing coals of the fireplace. In answer to my "God help," she made place for me before the fire. In a moment I was sitting beside her talking to her as though we were old acquaintances. Meanwhile, the man was grabbing a big armful of straw from his own pile and preparing a bed for the bookseller and myself in the other room. I cannot help remembering that bunch of straw. It makes the penny dole of a poor fellow equal to the gift of a Rockefeller. Christians, those peasants are by the strongest claim—natural disposition. That oft-repeated cry, "We must Christianize the foreigners," is like breaking into an open door.

To the woman I complained of the disorder and filth I saw everywhere among my people. "Why are all so dirty? Is it the same over in Russia?" She became animated. "Why! and boarders? How can you keep the house clean with twenty men to take care of, and children?" She had had four, one of whom had died, and she was not yet twenty-three. "Who keeps boarders over in the old country? Not to think of such a thing!" It was too obvious to ask her why Russians do it here. It is the only chance they have to accomplish the main purpose of their coming, which is to save money; an amount insignificant in America, perhaps, but large in a Russian village. Boarders and keepers; and for both sides it is bitter. The "hazda" receives $3 per month from each man. For this sum the latter is entitled to a lodging together with some fifteen other men. A neighbor had twenty-eight at one time, said the woman, in four rooms —the half of a company house—for which she paid $8. Each room was about twenty feet square.

The hazda attends to the washing of underwear and bedclothes, supplies cabbage for the soup, and does the cooking. She reaps some profit from the butcher, baker and grocer on the things she purchases for her boarders. Minor features in the unwritten constitution of keeping boarders are peculiar; the hazda herself, but not her man, has the right, free of charge, of taking part in the mess; so have her ungrown children. When the men wash after coming from work, she is supposed to wash their backs. Arduous task, undoubtedly, that of boarder-keeping. At the highest estimate, it can bring about $60 per month, if based on twenty boarders. With the husband making a little over this sum, I heard of a couple who had managed to amass $6,000 in five years.[7] They had had exceptionally good fortune, no doubt, up to that point—no seasons of non-employment, sickness or other losses. The husband then died, and although almost half of the money was spent on a tremendous drunken "pomin" (that heathenish survival of accompanying a burial with a carouse), and a gaudy monument in the cemetery, the wife returned to Russia a rich, envied widow, sure to find another husband.

---

[7] In this case possibly a clandestine selling of liquor helped.

"Say, do you have 'banyas' (bath-houses) there in Suvalki as they do in Great Russia?" "Oh, certainly, my father had a nice banya." So it is; even the poor peasant in north and middle Russia has, besides his "izba," a bath-house, as an American has a bathroom.

It is not a very elaborate affair; a room with a high bench built stepwise and a big water tub; hot stones from the fire-place in the anteroom are thrown into the tub to heat the water; others are be-sprinkled, producing an enormous amount of steam, which one can take in degrees of heat on the different steps of the bench. Invariably the bath is accompanied by a "birch broom" beating all over the body, thus intensifying the heat. The bather especially likes that taking-the-breath-away sensation. The amount of heat a peasant can stand by being beaten with birch twigs would take the breath away forever from many a more highly organized being! Steam and birch twigs remove dirt very effectively, without the use of soap. It is not to be contended that the peasant loves his banya solely for the sake of cleanliness; it is a pleasure to him. The saying that it is only in the third generation that the foreigner in America takes to the bath, is reversed in the case of Great Russians at least. It is the first generation that changes its habits; it stops taking the bath when it comes to America. A Moscow merchant would not see the insulting point if I should read to him what I saw in a Sunday newspaper not long ago, that he goes to bath once a year; why, he might as well be accused of not liking his vodka as of not liking his bath!

"Why don't you make the bath-houses here?" I asked my hostess, and she explained how much of an undertaking it would be. "Does your husband drink as much as the others?" I continued my inquiry. "Once in awhile; he does not spend much on drink." As a matter of fact, none spend much on drink. A keg of beer costs only $1 and that is sufficient for a good spree for five men. Most know when to stop. The expense comes later at the adjustment of the result of drinking; payment for battery and arrests. "Does your husband beat you?" "Doesn't beat, doesn't love," she answers in a Russian saying.

I nearly failed to notice the woman's children—three of them, sitting quietly not far from us, seemingly possessed of that "contemplative spirit of the East." The eldest, about ten years old, attended school, and spoke English as well as Russian. His father had already taught him to read in Russian.

I still had to provide a quilt and a bedcloth for the night on my straw bed. Again going from house to house, chance brought me first to an English-speaking family, where I was given to understand that I was crazy to ask such a thing—stranger as I was. I could not but agree with them, civilized as I had become, and would doubtless have acted as they did. But in an Old Believer's house, I got a quilt and a sheet just for the asking. The quilt was old and dirty, but the home-made linen cloth, fresh and clean, was exquisite.

Searching for my companion, I came across a group of Old Believers outside a house. Through the light which streamed from an open door I discerned standing with them a tall man, not very well shaved, with drooping mustachios, certainly an American. He proved to be a former Texas cowboy, now a farmer living on 12 acres of land in the vicinity of Wet Mines. I wondered that he kept company with my Old Believers and told him so. "Oh, they are as good as gold to me," said he. As I engaged in conversation with him, not as a Russian but just as a "decent-like furriner," his opinion could not have lacked sincerity. I found him, later on, sitting in an Old Believer's house, among a bearded crowd, drinking and jollying with them. For him they embodied the essential traits of a "white man"—no littleness, no stinginess; readiness to fight on provocation, redoubtable, too, in fight; the good-natured, cheerful disposition; and last but not least, the ability to drink like a fish without dying from it. Oh! if there were but common soil of intercourse with Americans for these Russians other than drinking!

I finally found my companion in an empty house surrounded by a crowd of young fellows who were poring over his case of books. Among them were four American boys. Bottles strewn on the floor made it clear that drinking was going on in this house, although with the exception of a red-headed fellow they called "Dutchman," who was rather piggish and obscene, I did not notice anybody behaving badly. All were busied with books. A nice-looking Russian youth was translating the inscriptions under the pictures in a book about the Russian-Japanese War to a refined, sympathetic American chap who might have been driven from a good position by bad times out of the city. The Russian youth talked to me with rapture about the joys of reading a book with the long title, Story About How a Lioness Has Reared a King's Son.

I found the Old Believers the most kind-hearted, good-natured lot of people I had ever met, almost childlike, despite their sometimes sullen looks, and I an asset, is it,—this kindness and good-nature, as qualities for a man to depend upon in the struggle for life? Yet, if the golden age should come, more of these qualities will be needed. The Romans could not imagine that any force but brute force counted. Nowadays the world believes that "brains" alone count. I do not wish to say that every casual American observer will find these men of such kindly disposition as I describe. Ignorance is suspicious, stubbornness is difficult to handle. And he is difficult, the Old Believer. Maybe, too, those good qualities of heart belong to men who have had to struggle only with nature, not with men, for their existence. I am told that here, under the ground, it comes often to ugly fights for cars. Through faulty organization in some of the mines, cars are not furnished promptly nor in sufficient number for the coal loaders. And Old Believers, it is said, prove more savage than anybody else in the contest to secure them.

In common with all Russians in America, these men are steady workers, despite their love of drink. "Drunkard and wise—two virtues in him." they are apt to say cynically about themselves. Their industry came rather as a surprise to me. We Russians of advanced thought often agree with the reactionaries in one thing, that the "muzhik" is lazy. "If he would not be so lazy there would not be famine; a big stick is good enough for him," says the reactionary. "If he were not so lazy, he could throw all that pile of corruption into Hades," say we. Overworked, the Russian peasant of course is not. Imagine in America a scene like this: A huge fellow lying on the ground in the market-place waiting for an employer. He may be asleep; all his concern is to expose the sole of his bare foot, on which is chalked the price he expects for his labor. Woe to the man who shall arouse him for bargaining!

Is there then real ability among them? you ask. Have any achieved success? To be sure, there is no railroad president among their number, but I know a heater-boss on the South Side, who is boss over five furnaces; he can make $130 to $150 per month. Now, to the ordinary reader this may seem of small account. But I know enough of steel making to assert that it is about as easy for an ordinary American college graduate to become a railroad president as for a Russian peasant to become a heater-boss. The work is skilled and the position is next to that of a roller-boss in responsibility.

The Old Believers show a remarkable weakness in their church organization, caused mainly by the ambiguous position of their priests. In the Greek church, ordination is a sacrament and can be performed only by a bishop. Now bishops can be appointed only by an assembly of bishops, and many Old Believers argue that the so-called "Austrian" bishops are not lawful and they recognize only the priests of the Orthodox church who come over to "old belief." Others either wrangle about their priests, or do not recognize any.

Out of the estimated 10,000 Russians in the state of Pennsylvania, in my opinion close to 3,000 are Old Believers.

Of these over 1,000 live in Allegheny County and the vicinity. Yet scattered as they are these people have only one prayer house (in Essen), and one priest —a peasant, quite like any member of his flock, without education, although undeniably a good, sober man. He was born a Prussian citizen and served in the Prussian Guards, with whom he was at Sedan in 1870 as a non-commissioned officer. Afterward he became a Russian, and worked as a small boss on government railroads. Now here he is a *primus inter pares* with the Old Believers. His six-foot-three, or thereabout, looks extremely sound, and no one would think him to be sixty-seven years old. This priest, however, does not seem to be generally accepted, and many marriages await a blessing in the old country. Lack of organization is generally a weak point with Old Believers; indeed, the worst thing I know about them is that they are not strong union men and they are accused of having broken up the longshoremen's union in Erie. I do not know whether or not this charge be true, but I do know that the derisive "ba, ba's" hurled at them must have been no small factor in any estrangement of the Old Believers from the rest of the workingmen.

If to me should be put the question that so persists in the discussion of any group of immigrants: Are they desirable, those long-bearded Russians? I am almost ready to say no. Not because of their drunkenness; this can be cured, and must be cured. Sweden, thirty years ago, was a land of drunkards; not so today. Not because of their crowded, inhuman living; this can be remedied by regulations similar to those that in time of war are posted on every freight box-car in Russia—"Eight horses or 40 men only." But rather because of the fact that so few wish to become American citizens. I cannot see how a group of men can be desirable in any country which they regard as a purgatory, be they ignorant Russians peasants in America, or highly skilled Belgian engineers in Russia.

Together with the rest of the Russians—for the matter of that, with the rest of the Slavs—these Old Believers live as though yet on passage, in steerage, "temporarily," without thought of adapting themselves to the conditions that surround them, still less of improving them. They expect to go back home. Patriotism has nothing to do with their return. It is a matter of personal expediency.

A similar phenomenon exists in Russia. Our small industrial force there is more than half composed of such hybrid contingents—peasants coming to the industrial centers "to make money for taxes," living in conditions as bad, though hardly worse than those in Pittsburgh. But here the parallel ceases, for though a Russian city is by no means a great center of culture, its civilizing influence on the hordes of peasants who flock to it is much more rapid and effective than is the case in America. Here in this great country of freedom and enlightenment the wall that encircles ignorance seems to be higher and more impregnable than that of China.

Still, if I noticed among my people any inclination to stay here, it was among these same Old Believers. Many have made the journey here two, even three times, and have lost attachment to their native soil. Perhaps these would not now become farmers. If when Old Believers first arrive they could be helped to settle in their primordial capacity of husbandmen, the United States would have in them a good agricultural element. Not that I believe my long-bearded countrymen to be human material inferior for whatever purpose to any other people coming to the United States. But undoubtedly it would be a hard task and a long one to turn into Americans, men who for two hundred years have preserved their Russian traits in Poland. Possibly decent, neighborly Americans—not merely reformers and social workers—could conquer Russian ignorance and superstition if they could overcome their own disgust at the "hideous looks and ugly cries" of the foreigners. So Marius conquered the Cymbrians and Teutons by making his soldiers first face the barbarians without fear. Yet, it can hardly be.

It is up to the Russians themselves to convert their unenlightened compatriots to "Americanism," not using the term in the European sense of shrewdness and agility, but as meaning what is good in civic life. There are already Russians in America fitted for such work. The revolution has sent over here many men who in their own country were ready to risk their lives to teach people how to live like human beings. Where are you? Some, as did Garibaldi, may be making candles for a miserable pittance, lost in dreams of returning home to fight. Others, indignant at themselves and at their countrymen for giving themselves up to selfish pursuits when they have known the service to principals, are denouncing America for all kinds of things. Here is a task for you, *Gde vy? ot-sovis!*

THE RUSSIAN MOLOKANS IN LOS ANGELES
1929

In an interesting sociological study,
Pauline V. Young of the University of
Southern California, described the main
characteristics of the Russian Molokan
community in Los Angeles. This group of
about 5,000 Russians belonged to a sect
in conflict with the Russian Orthodox
Church, and was forced to leave its native country because of religious persecutions. The group settled in Los
Angeles at the beginning of the twentieth
century.

Source: American Journal of Sociology,
vol. 35 (1929), pp. 393-402.

《The Molokan community in Los Angeles for over a quarter of a
century has struggled ceaselessly to maintain unimpaired the peculiar communal life and native cultural organization which it brought
from northern Caucausas. It is increasingly evident that the battle
is lost. The defenses of this group against the assimilation of the
younger generation are more powerful perhaps than those of any
other peasant known to American life. They have a long tradition
of social isolation, deeply rooted habits of collective action, social
customs which are backed by well-defined religious sanctions, intelligent native leadership, and a consciously developed and oft repeated determination to avoid contacts with a "sinful world."
Nevertheless, they are unable longer to maintain their cultural integrity and strikingly exhibit the effects of American urban life
upon native cultures. Their fate lends further weight to the thesis
that American city life permits no permanent segregation of cultures but invincibly fuses the most refractory social elements.》

Briefly, the Molokans are Russian peasants of unusually sturdy
physique and of strikingly dignified intelligent appearance. They
are religious sectarians. With a host of other sects, they dissented
from the Greek Orthodox church of Russia nearly three hundred
years ago. They refer to themselves as the "Spiritual Christians of

the Sect of Holy Jumpers." Their more common name, the Molokans, or the "Milk-drinkers," was given to them in contempt by
the Russian Orthodox clergy because the group after dissension
did not abstain from the use of milk and dairy products during
Lent.

Time does not permit us to review the complexities of the Russian schism.[1] Suffice it to say that it was the seed-bed in which Molokanism grew and throve; there were generated the interacting
forces which have determined the religious, social, and moral habits
and philosophy of the group. It is generally agreed by competent
students of the movement[2] that of all the numerous sects which
made their appearance at that time, the Molokans and their twin
sect, the Dukhobors, are the most rational in their principles, the
most conscientious in their religious practice, the most completely
unified group—a group whose strength of personality and "will to
differ" are unsurpassed even by the Quakers. However, they lack
scholarship and have no historical insight. They are prejudiced
against "worldly wisdom"; as a result of their "barren disputations
and primitive methods of controversy they have created for themselves a sort of crude scholasticism."[3]

The Russian church and state took an extremely hostile atti-
tude to the entire schismatic movement which fairly convulsed the
empire at the beginning of the modern era. The Molokans, along
with other sects, endured countless persecutions: exile into the
wilds of Transcaucasia, imprisonment, banishment to Siberian
mines, confiscation of property. Religious martyrdom is the basis
of a powerful tradition in this group. Indeed, so large a part does
their persecution play in their attitudes that they still seem to suffer
from a "persecution complex." They have compensated for their
inferior social position through strong communal unity, by religious
zeal, and by many of those personal and social virtues which are the
essential elements of a well-regulated social order. They soon be-

[1] See F. C. Conybeare, *Russian Dissenters;* also Leroy Beaulieu, *The Empire of
The Tzars and the Russians* (especially Vol. III), and A. Shchapov, *The Russian
Raskol* (Russian).

[2] Such as Haxhausen, Kostomarov, Leroy Beaulieu, and others.

[3] Leroy Beaulieu, *op. cit.,* p. 345.

came imbued with a passion for personal sacrifice; "their souls melted into a fraternity of souls,"[4] and as Spengler has pointed out "it is only through such grand instances of worldly passion which express the consciousness of a *mission* that we are able to understand those of grand spiritual passion, of dynamic charity."

For the sake of their religious ideals they have migrated half way around the globe. They hailed America as the land of destiny. They saw in it religious security, freedom from an arbitrary government, and an opportunity to live a life in harmony with their understanding of divine Law. Little did they anticipate the consequences of life in a modern metropolis and the inevitable influences of the American melting-pot.

They left Russia in large family groups, or *clans*, guided by a clear vision of the goal they sought. Six or seven thousand souls, comprising less than a thousand families, settled in Los Angeles in less than two years' time, about twenty-five years ago. They invaded a congested area of the city within walking distance of the downtown district, displacing for the most part immigrant Japanese.

The men found work almost immediately as unskilled laborers, their wives as domestics or "hands" in the fruit orchards. The older people upon arrival in the big city did not lose their social bearings. With poise and dignity and the inflexible logic befitting a Russian peasant, they renewed their "will to differ" and restating somewhat their philosophy they condemned the city's artificial social structure, its man-made laws, its sinful ways of living, and withdrew into their own group with revived faith in their own traditional beliefs. They continued practicing Molokanism with undeviating devotion to a triumphant Christianity. Their culture acquired a new moral direction and gained in motive power.

There is a certain idealism about the Molokan community which seeks to exemplify the early Christian principles of the "natural order of things" and to perpetuate the divine character of human institutions. "The Lord is our spirit and guide. God's law is the only law which must be obeyed. Law must be moral law, inner law" (an elder).

Thus they have crudely restated the Kantian moral law which

---

[4] Oswald Spengler, *The Decline of the West*, I, 349 f.

has its source and sanction in the very nature of men. They have thus established a kind of theocratic democracy in which they recognize no ministers, or bishops; all are equal by divine dispensation. Basing their teachings almost literally on the Scriptures every aspect of life is an object of religious attention; hence their chief institutions are religious. Indeed their only formal social organizations are the family and the church. Communal efficiency in the minds of the Molokans does not depend on number of organizations but on control through custom.

Custom has long imperiously regulated the social life of the Molokans. From the method of cutting their hair and the kind of food they eat to the manner of marrying their children and burying their dead the Molokans have persistently followed the footsteps of their forefathers. The lives of the older Molokans are so strongly systematized that the individual's principles and conduct rarely need to be consciously or forcibly regulated for him. Personal habits are prescribed and sanctioned by his religious code. Control through the folkways and mores extends to all details of his simple daily life.

The older Molokans are not stirred by the desire for personal achievement or by the hope of the attainment of individual success. They do not strive for social position or for economic advancement, which in an immigrant group may become almost an obsession. Their social hierarchy is based on age, personal merit, religious activity. They have never developed social classes, or castes.

The group well illustrates how potent a social force religion becomes among the masses in the rural environments once it has been thoroughly democratized and its adherents no longer delegate their religion to church functionaries, but hold themselves personally accountable for the performance of their religious duties.

In a group so intimately bound together it is inevitable that each member should participate in the religious activities and thinking of the group. Few peasant communities take as much time in rehearsing their history and tradition as the Molokans. Their quasi-spontaneous religious ritual is rich in feeling and full of the emotional tone of the southern Slav. Uplifted by a sense of the presence of the Holy Ghost they fall into ecstatic trances in which "jumping"

and "speaking with tongues" are the characteristic modes of behavior. The exchange of the "brotherly kiss" adds effectiveness to
their ceremonies and binds them together into a strong "we-group."

The Molokans have attained considerable success in their system of self-government and mutual aid. Their success may be partly ascribed to the efficiency and native intelligence of their elders.
The group is accustomed to follow its leaders and respond to their
call with the sensitivity and naïveté of the peasant sectarian. However, leadership is not arbitrary in the Molokan group. It arises
naturally on the basis of unity of sentiment and social habit. The
leaders are also presbyters and act as social reformers perpetually
active in the inauguration of a "heavenly city on earth."

The qualifications for leadership among Molokans are relatively simple: age, experience, practical efficiency, religious inspira-
tion, virtue—these are the paramount values. The Molokan leader
is the community personified. He in himself sums up the virtues
and aspirations of the group. Most elders can be readily recognized
in a crowd. They have an uprightness of bearing, a sharp, penetrat-
ing look, an efficiency and directness of action which command attention and respect.

It is difficult to explain such concepts as "organization," or
"community," to the Molokans as they associate these terms with
formal government, the rule of which they have traditionally re-
jected for their own group. They define the various social situations
which arise in the colony by discussion, by popular opinion and
group sentiment. The social opinion of the group is expressed
through gossip, by personal criticism of the younger by the older,
by appeal to tradition. It is formulated during their social and religious gatherings, festivals and conferences and other countless
spontaneous meetings characteristic of peasant life. "We have not
a single newspaper in any of our communities, and we don't need
any. News travels faster by word of mouth. And the 'living word'
carries deeper than the printed word."

The Molokans have now been in Los Angeles for nearly twenty-
five years and the first chapter in the history of their urbanization
can be written. For a long time the group failed to realize that by
their unwitting choice they had come to the very antipodes of their

former life. Village life in Russia had been personal and intimate, characterized by economic self-sufficiency and primary group organization and control. In America they faced a social-economic organization characterized by impersonal, anonymous, secondary relationships with an endless variety of strange activities, customs, and beliefs. Industry, school attendance, real estate agents, clever salesmen, public officials, social reformers, slowly and subtly penetrated the colony, lured their children into the outer world and gradually broke down the social isolation and cultural integrity of the group. The Spiritual Christians soon found themselves in the thick of "American materialism." They brought with them to America a set of social attitudes, values, and psycho-social traits which are the result of long-cherished sentiment, of habitual ways of action which cannot be discarded readily at will even under the most urgent circumstances of life. The whole process of adjustment of an immigrant group to American life involves not only an intellectual understanding of our ways of acting and thinking but it most frequently involves an uprooting of old habits, deep-seated emotions, and lasting sentiments. A stabilized group of older men and women are incapable of such a psychological transformation, and necessarily remain aliens. Their children due to the same psychological limitations cannot establish habits of acting, thinking, and feeling which would coincide with those of their elders. Each generation has a peculiar set of social experiences which determines its conduct habits. Conflict of cultures is a result of such polarity of social experience.

The younger generation of Molokans display the general "cultural temperament"[5] of their elders, greatly modified, however, by numerous daily contacts with American city life. School, recreation, industry, exert their influence at an early age. Life under these conditions gradually changes in content and philosophy, and the Molokan youth soon becomes the typical *cultural hybrid* characteristic of many immigrant groups; that is, he is not fully incorporated into either of the cultures which he represents.

The Molokan elders, however, due to an ardent desire to main-

[5] For an elaboration of this concept see Robert E. Park, "Education in Its Relation to the Conflict and Fusion of Cultures," *Publications of American Sociological Society*, Vol. XVII, 1918.

tain their traditional life and scheme of social control, have developed no mechanisms for dealing effectively with cultural hybridism. In an urban environment systematization of life and traditional behavior are cumbersome and highly ineffective. Still that is all the older generation understand and hence they are forced to a policy of passive resistance and aloofness in the face of the invasion of the strange culture. Strongly dominated by religious faith they have not developed mechanisms of coercion and persuasion of the young. They have appealed to the young to maintain their "glorious past." The young people have not responded to the appeal to tradition and religious principles. These ideals are now too abstract for these city-bred children. Culture is acquired through contact and participation, and vicarious experience does not readily and fully transmit attitudes and values or social reality. The young boys and girls among the Molokans have often expressed great curiosity as to their history, but the group traditions are fast becoming mere folk lore to them. The tales of martyrdom and persecution seem to them even too gruesome to repeat. They are affected by the emotional tone of the ritual but are greatly embarrassed by the ceremony of the "brotherly kiss." They are imbued with the presence of the Holy Ghost but they quit going to church as soon as "the Holy Ghost makes them jump." They consider it humiliating to jump and cannot reconcile this behavior with American practices and attitudes.

Living in social isolation the older generation have never developed a system of criticism or reflection upon established custom. The young people, however, reflect seriously upon their behavior in the light of the reactions of their American neighbors to whose attitudes they are sensitive.

You see, my parents read the Bible to me and tell me I must do as it's written. God gave you a mind, why don't you use it? Why don't you figure out the Bible for yourself? My mother says: "Keep still, child, you are ignorant, you must do as your forefathers did before you." Sure, it's all right, if you're going back to them old times. But I ain't going to—in this country [a young Molokan man].

The factors which assured the family unity of the older generation are no longer operative upon the young people. They have developed traits of personal initiative and ingenuity; they have acquired new skills and aptitudes and feel the need of making their own way in the world. Their elders are no longer the only people who exert influence upon them. Life is now infinitely more complex. They are responsive to a variety of institutions and form new and well-defined ideas of their duties and responsibilities. Not infrequently the young people are torn between two divergent standards. Hence, they become confused. In the conflict between the new and the old way of thinking and acting they find little help either at home or in the outside world since both the home and the larger community prescribe their own code and are indifferent or hostile to that of the other. Frequently a new and different mode of behavior emerges, subject to neither the old nor the new system of control. Some of the young people never make adjustments satisfactory to either group; they become demoralized, restless, mobile, delinquent. And as the age for marriage increases, as economic independence becomes harder to secure, and the insistence on prolonged school training is more strictly enforced, offenses become more frequent and more serious in character—their stabilization becomes more uncertain.

The failure of the Molokans to participate in the life and institutions of the larger community has resulted in indifference on the part of the city government with the result that the section of the city occupied by the colony is very poorly serviced, and many signs of communal deterioration are in evidence. Health problems, housing conditions, policing problems are becoming more and more acute in that district. Bootlegging has a strong hold in the community. Factories, warehouses, railroad yards are edging in closer and closer converting this residential section into a semi-industrial district. Cheap amusement houses are encroaching upon the puritanically spirited Molokan inhabitants. A mixture of races—Negroes, Mexicans, Armenians—with a variety of dialects and standards of living surround the Molokan colony on all sides. Still, the older Molokans have heretofore tried to maintain their spiritual brotherhood much as if they were in rural Russian isolation, closing their eyes, as it were, to everything surrounding them.

Yet this has proved impossible, for the "spiritual brotherhood," firm in its stand against Russian bureaucracy, is unable to withstand the influence of the city slum. They have come more recently to recognize the problems of their district; they quite properly regard it as an "infected area." The behavior of their children in the fascinating but bewildering city streets sorely perplexes them. They discuss the "degradation of their souls and their shameful, pagan conduct." When the elders get together these problems lead to much serious thinking and discussion. Little of practical consequence results since they have no experience or technique for dealing with such problems. When the situation becomes extremely aggravating they petition the school authorities, the police commission, the anti-saloon organizations. But their petitions have little effect since they come from a group of aliens, non-voters, "just Russians."

Under such circumstances the young people have discovered that it is possible to cross the line from Molokan to American life with comparative ease. Already a number have alienated themselves from their native culture and become "American." A few have even intermarried; others hope to do so.

There is a group of young people, however, who are still in large measure subjected to the force of Molokan communal influence. They have not yet acquired sufficient intellectual power and economic independence to emancipate themselves completely and break away from the customs which their parents hold sacred. The young people in all stages and periods of life generally show intense devotion to home ties. The familial bonds of affection and solidarity are still generally strong enough to bridge the cultural gap between the two generations. And this loyalty of the child to the family wins the parents' admiration and approval. And as economic independence of the younger people grows the parents give them greater and greater freedom and reluctantly confess admiration of their success in American life. The parents thus make many adjustments to the demands of their children and unwittingly begin to share in the more conventional American life. The process of adjustment to American life necessarily results in varying degrees of accommodation and assimilation. But every stage involves a new mode of conduct, a new philosophy of life. It is this individualized behavior which disintegrates traditional Molokan organization. The older group in Russia was effectively organized to carry on the religious struggle. Its very efficacy in maintaining itself against its Russian enemies makes it incapable of dealing with the forces which disintegrate their social organization in America. They are beginning to realize now they are helpless and incapable of assuming leadership over the younger people. The only escape they can suggest is flight from the city. But this "solution" does not appeal to the young people, nor indeed to any of the groups who have become rooted in the economic life of the city and habituated to it.

The colony at present displays the operation of several divergent social systems, which can almost be thought of as "constellations of social forces" superimposed upon or included one within another. Conflict is inevitable between the divergent modes of behavior. Unanimity of thought and simplicity of action are breaking down. The most dominant characteristics of primary group organization are unanimity of thought and simplicity and certainty of action. Yet with the establishment of reflective thinking and the development of new skills, division of labor and of personal initiative, systematization of behavior, unanimity, and simplicity are lost. And since these peasants lack specific techniques for dealing with urban problems traditional leadership functions ineffectively. Individualized behavior arises with the multiplying of social codes. The old structure is crumbling and losing its potency and nothing comparable is taking its place. The younger generation have not yet come into their own.

THE UNIVERSITY OF PITTSBURGH
RUSSIAN CLASSROOM
1938

On July 8, 1938 the Russian Classroom was
officially innaugurated at the University
of Pittsburgh, as one of the existing
eighteen international classrooms. The
room is an important tribute to the Russian
heritage in the United States, and has an
interesting history.

Source: The Russian Classroom. The Uni-
versity of Pittsburgh, Achievements of the
Nationality Committees and the Office of
Cultural and Educational Exchange, n.d.

Below an embroidered banner of St. George, patron saint of Moscow
since the fifteenth century, is a carved message announcing to American students sitting around the seminar table that, "Valorous youth is
victorious over forces of evil and darkness." The banner, appliquéd
with pieces of sixteenth and seventeenth century fabrics — brocade,
velvet, petit point —, hangs within the "kiot," a Slavic word for a
wall frame treated as a piece of furniture.

A dado, a low wainscot of simple open boards laid horizontally, runs
completely around the room. Opposite the kiot is the blackboard in
the shape of a triptych, a three-leaf frame which, in Orthodox churches,
supports the icons. The doors, when closed, display a grille of carved
wooden spirals over a flat ground of rich red velvet. The radiators
are covered with the same spirals over red velvet.

The seminar table is made of long slabs of oak, matched in contrasting grains, and held together by ornamental keys. The carved motifs on the apron of the table and the back of each student chair have
their origins in Russian folk ornaments. The back of each student chair
is of a Byzantine cruciform circle pattern, surmounted by a triangle,
each carved with the symbol of a different section of Russia — the
reindeer, the tundras, the fish, the Caspian Sea.

The professor's reading stand is ecclesiastical in character, and the
wrought-iron latches and plates on the blackboard and on the entrance
door are typical of Russian ecclesiastical metal work.

A jeweled icon, Our Lady of Vladimir, hangs above the corner
cupboard. The frame for this original seventeenth century piece was
hand-carved as a memorial to Dr. Avinoff, the designer of the room
and creator of the water colors.

BACKGROUND

For many centuries Russian art forms were influenced by the East, and there was little infiltration of either Gothic or Renaissance art. The Byzantine tradition, combined with indigenous ornamental forms, carried through all Russian art until long after the capture of Constantinople by the Turks in 1453. The Russian Orthodox churches with their predominantly Byzantine architecture and their magnificent decorative interiors were the treasure houses of the Russian people.

DESIGNER

Dr. Andrey Avinoff, director of the Carnegie Museum in Pittsburgh, designed the Russian Classroom. He was especially fitted to do so.

Born in Tultchin, southwestern province of Volhynia, Dr. Avinoff was the son of a family of the old nobility which in the fourteenth and fifteenth centuries ruled the commonwealth of Novgorod. His ancestors on his mother's side belonged to five different dynasties of Byzantium. He was an honorary judge and marshal of nobility of his district in the Government of Poltava when the World War broke out in 1914. Sent to the United States on official business for the Imperial Russian Government, he remained after the Bolshevik Revolution in 1917 and became an American citizen.

The carving is the work of Jan Luhowiak, a Ukranian who came to Pittsburgh before 1914 to carve altars in the Orthodox churches that were being built in this vicinity.

FORMS AND PATTERNS

The details of the carving on the furniture and throughout the room are designs which have come down from remote antiquity. Geometric in character are the carvings of truncated diamonds on the frame or kiot which enshrines the banner of St. George, of the cruciform pattern in the circles on the backs of student chairs, and of the spirals on the back of the professor's chair and on the blackboard grille. These geometric forms emphasize a sense of order and continuity. They belong to an ancient decorative tradition and are found in similar combinations in the art of very early cultures.

Floral patterns appear in the panels under the blackboard and on the corner cupboard. This is the sunflower, dear to the heart of the Russian peasant, and the symbol of the solar principle, the life-giving force. Many flowers in the decoration suggest, not the native plants of Russia, but exotic and imaginary flower forms of ancient Mesopotamia and Persia. The pot of flowers carved on both sides at the base of the kiot, or frame for St. George and the Dragon, comes from the Carpathian Mountains and the art traditions of Russians who migrated south from the Russian steppes over ten centuries ago.

THE FURNITURE

The seminar table is made of long slabs of oak matched in

contrasting grains and held together by ornamental keys. The carved apron is characteristic of massive tables in the Vologda district.

In the backs of student chairs and benches are the crosslike openings characteristic of furniture in the provinces of Vologda, Novgorod, Perm, and Yaroslav. Each chair has carved within the triangular space on the top rail a symbol of regional or stylistic significance. The sturgeon is the glory of Volga; the conventionalized lion is reminiscent of ancient Scythia; the reindeer typifies the northern tundras; the peacock, derived from an artistic conception of India, symbolizes immortality; the swan is the transformed princess from the folklore of Russian fairy tales.

In the triangle in the back of the professor's chair two birds adore the tree of life, symbolic imagery of a venerable tradition. The sacred tree with two worshiping birds or animals on either side has been used by many nations throughout different periods to portray fertility in nature.

The professor's reading stand, ecclesiastical in character, follows a model from Ouglitch. Its prototype in the Orthodox Church is the analoi used to support the heavy volume of Scriptures while it is read by the Deacon or Priest. The carving repeats motifs of the decoration.

The austerity of oak woodwork and white plaster walls is relieved by the red in the velvet cushions on the benches, in the velvet behind blackboards and radiator grilles, and in the velvet draperies which hang in folds from ceiling to floor on each side of the windows, traditional with seventeenth century decoration.

The blackboard is in the shape of a triptych, or three-leaved frame. In Russian Orthodox churches such frames are used to support the ikons, or painted holy pictures before the altar. Above the blackboard are carved the twin birds, Sirin and Alcanost, representing Joy and Sorrow.

THE VISHIVKA

The face and hands of St. George are embroidered to contrast the figure of the horse and the other details which are portrayed in applique of antique fabrics—brocade, velvet, petit point, damask. Most of these are pieces of sixteenth or seventeenth century fabrics purchased in Venice and Paris through the generosity of Miss Helen C. Frick. The hand emerging from the cloud in the upper right corner is the Divine Hand which guards youth against evil.

ORNAMENTAL HARDWARE

The strap hinges on the door are typically Russian. Their undulating lines, after a certain measure indicated by a decorative section, flow steadily to a magnificent symmetrical flower of Romanesque style. This represents the early oriental sources and the pagan era in Russia which merged into the Christian era. The wrought-iron hinges on the cupboard, with curved double joints, have the solid and simple shape of such fixtures on ancient Russian cupboards, especially in the Volga districts.

Grilles over the radiators are wrought-iron, intricate in design and elaborate in execution. The latches and plates on the blackboard, on the entrance door, and on the corner cupboard are characteristic of Russian ecclesiastical metalwork.

THE WINDOWS

The wooden frames of the Classroom windows are adorned with the somewhat octagonal flower stars which decorate the dado and the furniture. Design throughout the Classroom blends geometrical elements with life motifs. Consequently, the windows are of handmade glass in geometric shapes with bands of colored glass in seventeenth century motifs. Their colors pick up the raspberry and gold tones in the vishivka and sparkle with bright spots of ruby red and emerald green, suggesting the oriental jewelry so popular in pre-Petrovian Russia.

THE CORNER MOLDS

In Old Russia it was customary in the villages to make honey cakes in carved wooden molds. Honey cakes were particularly popular at Easter time. Dr. Avinoff adapted the general stylistic pecularities of such cake boards when he devised the idea of corner plaster molds representing the four seasons. Out of a quadrant of the sun emerges a conventionalized stem and plant—the grape for fall, the pine cone for winter, the bud for spring, and the sunflower for summer.

RUSSIAN GENERAL IN THE AMERICAN
CIVIL WAR RECALLED
1942

In a very well documented article, Albert
Parry sheds light on General John B. Turchin's life and military contributions
during the Civil War. Turchin, whose record left a story of competent leadership,
daring, sacrifice, pain, and glory, was
Lincoln's only Russian general.

Source: The Russian Review, vol. 1, no. 2
(April 1942).

I

O N A night in June 1901, an aged, broken man died in a hospital
for the insane in southern Illinois, and the next day the people
of Chicago read in a front-page obituary: "Veterans of the civil
war will recall with glistening eyes the deeds that made the old
commander's brigade famous."[1] Another newspaper printed a por-
trait of a proud and determined-looking man in a uniform of the
Union Army, with the caption: "Fighter Who Served Under Two
Flags."[2]

The other flag was that of Tsarist Russia. For John Basil Turchin
was born Ivan Vasilevich Turchaninoff,[3] and before changing his
name and gaining fame as a brigadier general in Lincoln's forces he
had attained the rank of colonel in the army of Nicholas I.

There were other Russians in the Union armies, but Turchin was
the only one with the rank, adventures, and troubles of a general.
Vladimir Magazinoff and some other sailors visiting America, deserted the Tsar's ships to enlist in the New York artillery and other
units of the North. A Russian officer, Colonel Charles de Arnaud,
took part in the campaign against the South from June 1861 to
February 7, 1862, when he was wounded. Prince Alexander Eris-

[1] *The Chicago Post*, June 19, 1901.
[2] *The Chicago Tribune*, June 20, 1901.
[3] The publisher's preface to John B. Turchin's *Chickamauga* (Chicago, 1888)
stated on page 5 that the General's original name was Turchininoff. *The Chicago
Tribune* for February 6, 1886, wrote: "His family name was Turchinoff, but after
emigrating to America he discovered that his name was too much for the average
Yankee to tackle. By degrees, or rather by syllables, terse Americans had abbreviated
the name of his forefathers until it was almost bereft of its identity. After each
syllable had been chopped off until nothing was left but "Turch," the greatly an-
noyed Russian put an end to further abridgement by announcing for the convenience
of his English speaking friends, he would cut off the tail, but he should draw the
line of demarcation at Turchin."

toff arrived in New York in 1862 and fought with the North for the principles of progress and freedom, although he was the owner of a tremendous estate in his native Georgia in the Caucasus.[4] Eristoff eventually returned home, but another Russian-born Union soldier stayed in America till his death many years later. Otto Mears was his name. He was born in Courland, Russia, of non-Russian stock, but left his homeland as a boy for San Francisco, where he enlisted as a youth in the First California Volunteers and saw Civil War service in New Mexico, and later became a well-known pioneer and road-builder of Colorado.[5]

But most of the fighting records of these volunteers were either brief or obscure. To this category belongs Prince Eristoff's. Some, like Mears, although coming to this land with no knowledge of English, were too young to remember for long either their Russian origin or their native tongue. To a historian, they are only technically Russians.

Turchin thus remains the best example of Russia's contribution to America's military effort. He was a soldier, not a mere boy, when he first came here. Affectionately and otherwise, he was known as the Mad Cossack (long before he actually went mad), and there was no mistaking him for anything but a Russian. Above all, he left behind him voluminous data, making his record in America a clear enough story of competent leadership, of daring and sacrifice, of pain and glory.

We have no direct evidence that Turchin was a Cossack, but it is certain that he was born in the province of the Don, on January 30, 1822. His father was a major in the regular army, a nobleman of well-off circumstances. After three years of elementary schooling, young Ivan was sent for three more years to a *gymnasiya* in Novocherkassk, from which, according to one account, he entered the artillery academy in St. Petersburg. Another version has it that upon completing his preliminary education the boy entered a cadet-school in St. Petersburg, from which—and not from the artillery academy —he was graduated in 1841 into the horse artillery service of the Tsar. He was nineteen, and an ensign. His schooling by then had included mathematics, gunnery, engineering, ballistics, military tactics, and mechanics, both theoretical and practial. He took part in the

[4]For information on Magazinoff, de Arnaud, and Prince Eristoff I am indebted to my friend Alexander Tarsaidzé and the manuscript of his forthcoming book, *Tsars and Presidents* (in collaboration with Roger Dow). Incidentally, Mr. Tarsaidzé is a grandnephew of Prince Eristoff.

[5]*Dictionary of American Biography*, Vol. XII, New York, 1933, pp. 485-86.

Hungarian campaign of 1848-49, and upon his return entered the
military academy for the general staff, "where he received a thorough training in advanced tactics, military history of campaigns,
topography and geodesy, military statistics, and military administration, graduating with high honors in 1852 and receiving as a reward
of merit the silver medal, which is presented to graduates passing the
highest examination."[6] It was then, at the age of thirty, that Turchin
was appointed to the staff of the Imperial Guards "as sub-captain,"
and within a few years was promoted first to captain, then to
colonel.[7]

It appears that he attained the rank of colonel in the Crimean
War of 1854-56.[8] In March 1854, in company with a naval officer,
Turchin was sent to survey the coast of the Gulf of Finland between
St. Petersburg and Narva to see whether the British and the French
could land their forces there in order to march on the Tsar's capital.
He suggested fortifications and other measures, and his recommen-
dations were adopted. Later in the war, Turchin was sent with a reserve army to Poland, for an Austrian invasion was seriously feared.
The end of the war found him there, restless and dissatisfied. He
was ordered to Moscow, to prepare quarters for the troops coming to
the old capital for the coronation of Alexander II. Instead, he reported ill and obtained a year's leave. The spa of Marienbad in
Austria was supposed to be his destination, but it was to England
that Turchin and his young wife went. From there, in the summer
of 1856, the pair sailed for the United States, arriving in New York
in mid August.

Why did Turchin leave Russia, never to come back? A Chicagoan,
who wrote while Turchin was still alive, had this explanation to
offer:

> During the long campaign in Poland, Colonel Turchin had grown tired of
> military service under the Russian Government, and had resolved to cut away from
> it at the earliest opportunity. Although at that time he had never crossed the Russian
> borders, he had read and heard a great deal of the land of freedom on the other side
> of the world, and the more he read and heard the more eager he became to leave
> the land of tyranny and despotic rule. To do this meant to abandon the brilliant
> career which was open to him; but freedom of thought, freedom of speech, free-
> dom of action were looked upon as of far greater importance than all the honors and
> military distinguishment which a capricious Czar might heap upon a service subject.[9]

[6]*The Chicago Tribune*, February 6, 1886.
[7]Turchin, *Chickamauga*, p. 5.
[8]*The New York Tribune*, June 20, 1901.
[9]*The Chicago Tribune*, February 6, 1886.

This was a time of unrest among the young men of Russia, yet
there was hope, too, that the new Tsar would begin to institute re-
forms, as indeed he soon did. Turchin's reason for going abroad was,
it would seem, not only a lofty thought of liberty but also a lusty desire for adventures.

He and his wife knew several languages, but no English. They
had some money, however, Madame Turchin being the possessor of
a small fortune, and with this they bought a farm on Long Island,
some thirty-five miles from Brooklyn. A year later the newcomer
felt that he knew the language well enough to venture upon new
horizons. Selling the farm, the Turchins moved to Philadelphia
where John enrolled in a college of engineering. Through one of
the teachers he met Alexander D. Bache, great-grandson of Ben-
jamin Franklin, and superintendent of the United States Coast
Survey. Bache liked the Russian's writings on scientific subjects, and
for a time Turchin worked for him—at little or no compensation,
due to Congressional reluctance to grant Bache additional funds.[10]

Work in private employment appeared to offer better terms. Tales
of the West with its wider opportunities and a more exciting way of
life attracted the Russian couple. In 1858 they moved to Mattoon,
Illinois, an up-and-coming town of 150 buildings with many more
on blueprints. Turchin was engaged as an architect to help with the
new construction. His Americanization was rapid, and he joined the
newly formed Republican Party, remaining a zealous member till
his death decades later. In 1859 Turchin took his wife to the young,
raw, sprawling, bustling city of Chicago where he accepted the position of a topographical engineer with the prosperous and evergrow-
ing Illinois Central Railroad.[11]

In those days it was natural for army men to alternate between
military service and pioneering work on railroads. Transport by rail
was as yet too new to develop schools of its own, while army officers
had enough knowledge of topography and machinery to be enticed
from their service to build and run the novel iron-horse.[12] The
Illinois Central had on its staff several men of military training and
future fame, among them the man who within a few years was to

[10]*Ibid.*

[11]*The National Cyclopaedia of American Biography*, Vol. XII, New York, 1904,
p. 241.

[12]The St. Petersburg-Moscow railroad, completed a few years before the Crimean
War, was built by that half-forgotten American army man and railroad-expert,
Major George Washington Whistler, father of the famous painter. See Albert Parry,
Whistler's Father, New York and Indianapolis, 1939.

emerge as one of the most talked-of leaders of American arms—Major General George B. McClellan. Indeed, there may be some connection between Turchin's coming to work for the Illinois Central and the fact that in 1855 McClellan had been sent to Russia by the United States War Department to study the lessons of the Crimean War.[13]

Turchin was later to recall the long conversations on the art of war he and McClellan used to hold in the offices of the Illinois Central where the Russian found the American as the chief engineer and vice-president of the railroad. Later, General Nathaniel P. Banks took McClellan's post with the road, and Turchin and Banks would discuss military problems for hours on end. All three were soon to find themselves on America's battlefields, putting to practical test some of their pet theories.

II

In April 1861 the news of firing on Fort Sumter reached the streets and prairies of the Middle West. Chicago buzzed with talk and indignation. Nathaniel Banks burst into the Illinois Central offices shouting that an army of one million men would have to be raised at once to push the rebels into the Gulf of Mexico. Taking down from the walls their maps of the United States, he and Turchin planned the campaign, while, outside, volunteers thronged the armories, regiments were formed, and commanders sought for.

On May 16 Banks departed, having obtained his commission as a major general. Meantime the Nineteenth Illinois Volunteers heard from Joseph R. Scott, their commander, that he was willing to step aside in favor of a more experienced officer. A deputation waited on Turchin, and he accepted immediately. On June 17, 1861, he received his official commission as a colonel in the United States service, to lead the Nineteenth Illinois. Scott remained with him as his lieutenant colonel.

Portraits of Turchin at this time of his life show a broad Slavic face, with intense eyes, hair beginning to recede into a high forehead, and a moustache and beard of moderate proportions. His admirers were to remember this "flaxen-haired Russian" as a man of "a striking physiognomy," whose photographs generally failed "to reflect the fire of his pale-blue eyes and the intellectual cast of features that characterize this distinguished soldier."[14]

[13]*Dictionary of American Biography*, Vol. IX, New York, 1935, pp. 581-82.
[14]*The Chicago Tribune*, February 6, 1886.

At Camp Long near Chicago, where Turchin joined his new regiment, he found over one thousand officers and men of the Nineteenth formed into ten companies. Six companies were made up of Chicago men, many of whom were sons of the city's best families. Four companies were composed of men from all over Illinois, with a number of sturdy farmers from the northern counties. Some of the companies had been drilled for years and had known war service for months, for they were part of such old-time organizations as the Highland Guards, Chicago Zouaves, and other groups of citizens who had believed in preparedness ever since the late eighteen fifties and had been in the active army since the fateful April, 1861. Turchin had good material to begin with, and now he told these men that their regiment was to become the best in the United States. Drill and more drill was the order of the day until, on July 12, 1861, the Nineteenth struck its tents and marched through the cheering crowds of Chicago to the depot. Mrs. Turchin accompanied her husband.

The first assignment was to Quincy, whence Turchin's men crossed the Mississippi River to the Missouri towns of Palmyra and Hannibal. There were to relieve the Twenty-first Illinois, then commanded by an obscure colonel named Ulysses S. Grant. Here Turchin had his first tiff with his superior, Brigadier General Stephen A. Hurlbut. He complained of the lack of uniforms and munitions, and would not fight until these arrived. Hurlbut stormed, but Turchin was obstinate and got what he wanted. From then on, Turchin's regiment guarded railroad bridges and struck at secessionists in the region, chasing away their newly formed units, destroying their barracks and seizing their provisions, organizing loyal citizens into home guards, and otherwise behaving "in the best possible manner."[15] Brigadier General John Pope, Hurlbut's chief, came to Palmyra to threaten the Russian with court-martial for allowing his soldiers to molest citizens' property, but Turchin protested that they took provisions only, as the food furnished his troops was of "the rankest kind"—nothing but "wormy hardtack and execrable salt junk."[16]

The regiment was next moved to St. Louis, then to Kentucky. It searched for the enemy, and it drilled. Mrs. Turchin was with the troops, as usual. In mid September orders came to entrain for Washington, to join the Army of the Potomac—but the Nineteenth never

[15] J. Henry Haynie, ed., *The Nineteenth Illinois; a memoir of a regiment of volunteer infantry famous in the Civil War of fifty years ago for its drill, bravery, and distinguished services*, Chicago, 1912, p. 140.

[16] *The Chicago Tribune*, February 6, 1886.

arrived. On the night of the seventeenth, in two trains, the regiment was crossing a bridge beyond Vincennes, Indiana, when the structure crashed under the weight of the second train. Six cars fell into the river; twenty-five men, including a captain, were killed; 105 others were injured, seven of them dying soon afterward in the hospitals of Cincinnati, and a few remaining crippled for life. Company I, mostly men from Galena, known as "anti-Beauregardists," suffered most. The Colonel and his lady labored with the rescue crews, he chopping with an axe the car-frames to release the crushed men, she tearing her skirts into bandages and ministering to the wounded. At a subsequent meeting of the citizens of Galena, the mayor of that city, Robert Brand, reporting on the accident, exclaimed that "when the dead, dying and mutilated lay in one mass of ruin; when the bravest heart was appalled, and all was dismay, this brave woman was in the water, rescuing the mangled from a watery grave . . . , a fit consort for the brave Turchin in leading the gallant sons of Illinois to battle!"[17] The Colonel himself was sad: "I am an old soldier, but never in my life have I felt so wretched as when I saw, by moonlight, my dear comrades on the miserable pile of rubbish . . . and heard the groans of agony."[18]

In Cincinnati, in Louisville, and finally in Elizabethtown, Kentucky, the regiment nursed its wounds and received new munitions and recruits. Among the latter there was a certain Alexander Smirnoff of Ottawa, Illinois, who had enlisted on September 25.[19] A Russian, judging by his name, he was perhaps attracted by his compatriot's fame and wished to serve under him while fighting for the Union.

Elizabethtown was semi-rebel, semi-loyal, and it was the job of the Nineteenth to bring the town and vicinity more firmly into the camp of the Stars and Stripes, while improving its own training. "Here we remained," wrote the historian of the regiment, " . . . securing information as to the manual of arms, guard mounting, picket duty, and battalion movements. Verily, Colonel Turchin and his subordinate officers were an energetic group of leaders."[20] On the press of *The Elizabethtown Democrat*, whose owners had conveniently fled, Turchin's men published *The Zouave Gazette*, to

---

[17]A. T. Andreas, *History of Chicago, from the Earliest Period to the Present*, Vol. II, Chicago, 1885, p. 181.

[18]J. Seymour Currey, *Chicago: Its History and Its Builders*, Vol. II, Chicago, 1912, pp. 110-11.

[19]Haynie, *The Nineteenth Illinois*, p. 93.

[20]*Ibid.*, p. 146.

which the Colonel himself contributed his sensible proclamations to the populace, also his articles for the soldiers on outpost duties, regimental bands, bugle signals, and other matters. William B. Redfield of *The Chicago Evening Journal* edited this unique paper, published "as often as circumstances will permit" (actually, every seven or eight days). The *Gazette* was full of lively items, and it sold briskly in camp and town and even in Louisville. Two Pennsylvania regiments, stationed near by, regularly bought several hundred copies.[21]

It was at this time that Turchin wrote and published a pamphlet entitled *Brigade Drill,* said to be the best of its kind since the old *Scott's Tactics.* The fame of Turchin's drill was spreading steadily, and citizens of Elizabethtown, both unionists and secessionists, but particularly young women, came to the grounds to marvel at the men's smart maneuvers. Turchin's "Russian methods, crossed with American patriotism, soon made that regiment a shining light of discipline and efficiency."[22] On his visit to the town in November, Turchin's new commander, Brigadier General Don Carlos Buell, was much impressed with what the Russian had done, saying to the Colonel: "I have never seen a better drilled regiment than yours."[23] A West Pointer, Buell was a stickler for drill and discipline.

Soon afterward, without raising him in rank, Buell gave Turchin a brigade. This was the Eighth Brigade, Army of the Ohio, under the divisional command of Brigadier General Ormsby M. Mitchell. Turchin, still a colonel, now led four regiments: Nineteenth and Twenty-fourth Illinois, Eighteenth Ohio, and Thirty-seventh Indiana, all infantry. Occasionally he had the use also of some artillery and cavalry. From December to February the brigade was at Camp John Quincy Adams, at Bacon Creek in Kentucky, and a rainy, miserable winter it turned out to be—for many, their first winter under canvas. There were long weeks of inaction, and illness was rife.

On February 10, 1862, Buell's army began to move southward, Turchin's brigade in the vanguard. Due to Grant's victories at Forts Henry and Donelson, the rebels under General Albert Sidney Johnston were in retreat before Buell. They were burning supplies and breaking bridges to hamper the Northerners, but, thanks to

[21]Copies of *The Zouave Gazette,* October-November 1861, are extremely rare now. I am grateful to the Chicago Historical Society for the opportunity to consult the first four issues of the *Gazette* in its possession.

[22]*The Chicago Record-Herald,* June 20, 1901.

[23]Haynie, *The Nineteenth Illinois,* p. 159.

Turchin's use of a big flat-bottom ferry which his scouts had found near an old flour-mill, the Nineteenth was the first to enter Bowling Green and seize much booty. Crossing into Tennessee, Mitchel's division, with Turchin's brigade still one of its most active parts, occupied Nashville late in February and Murfreesboro on the twentieth of March. Bridge building and skirmishes kept the brigade busy, and Turchin found time to offer to General Buell what the Colonel's admirers termed "most valuable strategical advice at Corinth."[24] Mrs. Turchin helped in the wagon ambulance, contributed by the grateful citizens of Chicago, and there is this memento of her work decades later: "Dear Madame Turchin! how we all respected, believed in, and came to love her for her bravery, gentleness and constant care of the sick and wounded. . . ."[25]

Early in April, while Grant (by now, of course, a general) fought and retreated at Shiloh; and while Buell and Grant drove the rebels back to Corinth, Turchin's brigade was sent over the tortuous roads to seize Huntsville in Alabama and thus cut the Confederates off from their direct communications with the east and southeast. The raid was a complete success, and Turchin was praised for it. He was now sure of promotion in rank, but before he could receive this honor an unpleasant thing happened.

The Eighteenth Ohio had been left by Turchin in occupation of Athens, Alabama, and early in May the regiment was overwhelmed by a rebel force. It was claimed that the rebels treated the Ohioans most savagely, taking few prisoners but shooting nearly all who fell into their hands. Outraged by the news, Turchin hastened to Athens with the bulk of the brigade, met on the road the retreating survivors of the Ohio regiment, and together with them retook the town. The annalist of the Nineteenth admitted: "In the midst of the confusion that accompanied and followed this affair some unsoldierly things were done by men of the brigade."[26] Some excused the retaliation by saying that the inhabitants of Athens had sniped at the Ohioans during their retreat and had abused them in other ways, too; and that anyway the reports of revenge by the brigade upon its return were grossly exaggerated. There was, for instance, no rape of the inmates of a female seminary near Athens, as charged at the time by the secessionists.[27]

[24]*The Chicago Record-Herald*, June 20, 1901.
[25]Haynie, *The Nineteenth Illinois*, p. 132.
[26]*Ibid.*, p. 166.
[27]T. M. Eddy, *The Patriotism of Illinois, a record of the civil and military history of the state in the War for the Union*, Vol. I, Chicago, 1865, p. 336.

Complaints reached General Mitchel that Athens had been sacked by the Mad Cossack's troops, and Turchin's superior hurried to the scene. Mitchel addressed the town folk, bidding them to organize a committee of inquiry. Turchin was to make an investigation of his own. When the reports were in, no charges were preferred. "General Mitchel was satisfied, but not so General Buell. . . Urged by field officers who were probably jealous of the 'Russian,' Buell caused Turchin to be placed under arrest, and a court-martial was appointed to try him."[28]

III

General James A. Garfield (later President of the United States) headed the court-martial which met in July, first in Athens and later in Huntsville. According to a newspaper account of the time, the main accusation was that Turchin "gave a silent consent to the perpetration of a series of outrages in which persons and property were alike disrespected." Neglect of duty, conduct unbecoming an officer and gentleman, and disobedience of orders were the three official counts against him. The charges described Turchin's soldiers as "Pillaging houses, plundering stores, forcing trunks, iron safes and wardrobes, destroying thousands of dollars in notes on hand, burning goods, carrying off silver plate and jewelry, watches and money, and last of all, committing an indecent outrage on the persons of two servant girls." Turchin himself "contracted debts and refused to liquidate them," also would not "enforce his authority" to prevent his troops from evil-doing, and disobeyed orders from the headquarters "in allowing the village to be plundered."[29]

Turchin pleaded not guilty to all the allegations except one—and that was the charge that contrary to regulations he allowed his wife to be with him at the front. Great crowds were attracted to the court rooms by the trial, and while certain persons were reported to be full of hatred for the Russian and eager to hear him judged guilty, others —especially his soldiers—were dismayed by the proceedings and muttered darkly. They said that Turchin was being tried by pro-slavery men for his anti-slavery sentiments. They were incensed when the court at last reached its verdict. It was a verdict of guilty and a sentence of dismissal from the United States Army.

During the trial, and while the findings of the court were on their way to Washington for confirmation, a section of the American press

[28]Haynie, *The Nineteenth Illinois*, p. 167.

[29]Correspondence from Athens, Alabama, to *The Cincinnati Gazette*, July 13, 1862, quoted in *The Chicago Tribune*, July 25, 1862.

shared the soldiers' feelings. *The Nashville Union* was quoted by *The Chicago Tribune* on August 2 that, because of the time taken by Garfield, Buell, and others to try Turchin, the very deliverance of East Tennessee from the rebels was being postponed—these generals were too busy judging the Colonel to fight the Confederacy! *The Chicago Tribune* thundered on August 2, 1862:

> Turchin's offense consists in believing that peace and war cannot be carried on successfully at the same time and place. He is not the man to allow his soldiers to die of scurvy for want of vegetables while guarding the onion patch of a traitor, and it does not lie in the boots of Don Carlos Buell to restrain him from hitting a rebel's head wherever he sees it.

In another editorial, on August 8, *The Chicago Tribune* applauded "the noble conduct of Colonel Turchin at his trial, his dignity, patience, his soldierly and manly bearing throughout." It echoed Turchin's words: "We hope that court-martial has not been altogether in vain." The editor called upon President Lincoln and the War Department to meet the court's sentence with proper indignation. He was supremely confident that the sentence would be reversed.

Meanwhile, President Lincoln and his War Department had their answer ready. The news was most surprising to all and extremely pleasing to Turchin and his friends: it was a commision promoting the Rusian to the rank of brigadier general!

Dated July 17, 1862, it coincided with the sittings of the court-martial. Made public after the sentence had been sent to Washington for confirmation, it had the effect of vindicating or at least forgiving Turchin. Officially, it was his reward for the capture of Huntsville. Now that he was promoted, Turchin's condemnation by a court-martial had to be set aside, for most of his judges sitting under General Garfield were colonels, who certainly could not judge a brigadier general.

His wife had gone back to Chicago, and now Turchin journeyed to rejoin her. Thousands of citizens accompanied Mrs. Turchin to the depot to meet the vindicated hero. They greeted the Russian with a tremendous ovation, and took him to Brand Hall, where they "tendered him such a reception that all doubts were set at rest as to what Chicago people thought of Buell's treatment" meted out to their man.[30]

Turchin's triumph was complete.

[30] *The Chicago Tribune*, February 6, 1886.

IV

Yet, he remained away from the major battlefields of the Republic for quite a few months. Possibly he did not want to return while his enemy Buell was still in charge.

But from October 1 to 8, the battle of Perryville was fought and lost by Buell—lost in the sense that he needlessly permitted General Bragg's Confederates to slip from his grip. For this Buell was dismissed in favor of Major General William S. Rosecrans. A thorough reorganization of the Army of the Ohio followed, and presently it became the Army of the Cumberland led by new commanders. Late in December and early in January it met the rebels in the bloody battle of Stone River, which both sides claimed as a victory but which actually ended in the Southerners' withdrawal. The Nineteenth Illinois distinguished itself in the battle, but among the fallen was Colonel Scott, Turchin's friend and successor as head of the regiment. Scott was seriously wounded while leading his men in a charge. Taken back to Chicago, he never recovered, dying months later, in July. There is a mention of General Turchin's part in the battle of Stone River,[31] but this seems to be in error. In fact, it was not until March 1863 that Turchin rejoined the forces in action.

Rosecrans first offered Turchin the Second Division of cavalry in the Army of the Cumberland, but Turchin said he disliked leading mounted men—a strange bias in a man born among Cossacks, if not a Cossack himself! Instead he took the Third Brigade of the Fourth Division. He found in his command the Eleventh, Thirty-sixth, Eighty-ninth, and Ninety-second Ohio, and the Eighteenth Kentucky regiments of infantry. Neither the famous Nineteenth nor any other Illinois regiment was now under him, but the troops from his state continued to follow his fortunes and cheer his name.

In later years Turchin was wont to consider 1863 as the turning point of the entire Civil War. His own outstanding share in that year of decision, he felt, had been in the battle of Chickamauga on September 19-20 and of Missionary Ridge on November 25, the two victories which gave to the Union the final control of Chattanooga and Knoxville.

At Chickamauga, General Turchin initiated bold bayonet charges. On one occasion, in a headlong charge, Turchin's "impetuosity carried him far into the rebel lines, and he was almost instantly surrounded by the rebel hordes, but the stout old Russian had no thought of surrendering." He turned back to the Federal lines, cutting

[31]*The National Cyclopaedia of American Biography*, Vol. XII, p. 241.

through with his men and "actually bringing with him three hundred prisoners."[32] He led not only his brigade but gave advice and encouragement to other troops. His horse was shot from under him, and he ran through a stubble-field signaling to his troops.·He cursed other generals, particularly when one of them, James B. Steedman, borrowed the Eighty-ninth Ohio from Turchin and left a number of these soldiers, together with some of his own, to be surrounded and captured by the rebels. It was at Chickamauga, on the second day of the battle, that Alexander Smirnoff was killed. In the two years since his enlistment this Russian soldier had been promoted to corporal and sergeant, all in the same Company C, Nineteenth Illinois, which at Chickamauga fought outside Turchin's brigade but close by.

At Missionary Ridge, Turchin led his units in scaling the height. He was at the extreme and thus most strategic left of the storming line. Nine guns were captured, and the rebels were pushed north even before other brigades could come to Turchin's aid.

The victory of Missionary Ridge opened Sherman's way to Atlanta. In that famous march to the sea, Turchin fought as far as the Chattahoochee River, six miles within sight of the Atlantic Ocean. In years to come he was recognized as one of the leaders in that particular campaign.[33] In May 1864, realizing that the three-year term of enlistment of the Nineteenth was drawing to its close, and the regiment was soon to be disbanded, he asked for its transfer to his brigade. His men said that he thus wished to show his abiding love for the men of the Nineteenth. By that time, only fifteen officers and 239 men remained in the regiment. In addition to the Nineteenth, Turchin's brigade in its last phase held the Twenty-fourth Illinois, the Eighty-second Indiana, Twenty-third Missouri, and Eleventh, Seventeenth, Thirty-first, Eighty-ninth, and Ninety-second Ohio, altogether nine regiments.

The Nineteenth was mustered out in June 1864, and those men who did not re-enlist to serve in other regiments were taken by train back to Chicago. In the same summer Turchin suffered a sunstroke, and went home on a leave of absence, "during which time, seeing that the Confederacy was going to splinters, he resigned his commission."[34] The exact date of his retirement was October 4, 1864.

[32]Eddy, *The Patriotism of Illinois*, Vol. II, Chicago, 1866, p. 51.

[33]Turchin's photograph appears in the group of "prominent leaders in the Army of the Cumberland and the Tennessee in Sherman's masterly movement to the heart of Georgia," published in Francis T. Miller, ed., *The Photographic History of the Civil War*, Vol. X, New York, 1911, p. 91.

[34]*The Chicago Tribune*, February 6, 1886.

He was forty-two years old, and full of vigor. To quote a description given of him at the time:

General Turchin is a man of medium stature and strong frame, slightly inclined to corpulence, with a massive well-formed head, and a face full of intelligence. His countenance is very expressive and betokens the union of a rare and delicate humor with great inflexibility of will and decision of purpose. He is impulsive, full of energy, thinks and acts quickly, and is rarely placed in that position where he cannot muster resources to meet its emergencies.[35]

V

Settled in Chicago with his wife once more, Turchin announced that he intended to be useful to his adopted country by reviewing the errors he had seen in the army. "If our language is sometimes harsh or cutting," he warned, "our intentions are honest, and we hope that our pamphlets will be patiently perused by the public." He thus prefaced his first pamphlet, in which he took to task Generals Mc-Clellan, Buell, and even Sherman; lamented the supply organization in the Union Army; discussed politicians and the army; drew comparisons between the emancipated negro and the Russian serf; and proposed a way of dealing with the "possible interference of England and France."[36]

But pamphleteering and writing in general did not take all of Turchin's time. He kept himself busy as a solicitor of patents until 1870 and then turned back to his old profession of engineering. Two years after the great fire he decided to move to the countryside, and so, in 1873, proposed this deal to the Illinois Central: he would establish a Polish colony in the southern part of the state, in Washington County, on some barren lands belonging to the railroad. The plan was accepted, and the General advertised among the Poles of Chicago, Detroit, and other Midwestern cities, tempting them with surcease from their factory labors. At a point 300 miles south of Chicago, a station on the railroad was established and called Radom after the city in Poland. The lands around were covered with dense timber, and these were now cleared to make farms of forty and eighty acres each. By 1886, nearly 500 Polish families had built their houses in this region, log affairs with interior walls plastered with a mixture of clay and lime in the old-country style. Wheat was raised, and the station of Radom became a village of more than 100 inhabitants and two stores, two blacksmith shops, one saloon, one

[35]Eddy, *The Patriotism of Illinois*, Vol. I (1865), p. 340.

[36]John B. Turchin, *Military Rambles*, Chicago, 1865. Copies of this pamphlet are rare by now, as most of them very likely perished in the great Chicago fire of 1871. For this article I studied the copy owned by the Chicago Historical Society.

large frame church, and a solid-looking school. Two Catholic priests and two sisters of charity were the leaders of the community.

In compensation, Turchin received from the Illinois Central a farm of eighty acres, half a mile from the village. At first he tried to raise crops himself, but soon rented out the land, although continuing to live in his farm house. He read and he wrote, and played his violin which he said was a Brescia made by Gaspare de Salo, some 250 years earlier. Occasionally, the General and his lady rode to Chicago to see friends and deliver a lecture or two. In the press of the time we find, for instance, a notice of his appearance at the Central Music Hall in February 1886 to deliver a talk on "The Battle of Missionary Ridge." In November 1888, together with several other retired generals, Turchin was invited by the War Department to come to Chattanooga, thence to proceed to the old battlefield of Chickamauga, and help correct the Department's historic maps of the great battle by indicating the positions of the troops. He enjoyed the trip and work immensely. In the same year 1888, the Fergus Printing Company of Chicago published Turchin's *Chickamauga,* a book of nearly 300 pages and eight maps.[37]

In that valuable if acrimonious volume, also in his interviews with newspapermen, the grey and long-bearded but sprightly General berated his colleagues and superiors of a quarter-century back in no uncertain terms. His old friend McClellan was an indecisive and vacillating flounderer, a very good engineer who could never make a great general.[38] Of Banks, Turchin said that "he was one of the most cordial, generous and open-hearted men I have ever met," but that it was too bad Banks was consumed with an ambition to lead troops when "he would have made the best Commissary General of any man in the country."[39] General Henry W. Halleck, according to Turchin, was a mediocrity, an empty braggart, and intolerable in his conduct toward his subordinates.[40] He quoted others in praising his, Turchin's courage, but censured them for not mentioning the movements of his brigade often or correctly enough. He cited Russian folk proverbs, and he referred, by comparison, to the battles

[37]This was published as Volume I of the series entitled "Noted Battles for the Union during the Civil War in the United States of America, 1861-65," and an advertisement promised the following volumes by General Turchin: II. *Battle of Missionary Ridge,* III. *Experiences and Impressions during the War of the Rebellion,* and IV, *Sketches of Russia.* For reasons unknown, *Chickamauga* was the only volume of the series ever published.

[38]Turchin, *Chickamauga,* p. 13; *The Chicago Tribune,* February 6, 1886.

[39]*The Chicago Tribune,* February 6, 1886.

[40]*Chickamauga,* pp. 13-14 and 49.

of Borodino and Sevastopol, in discussing America's Civil War and just how it should have been properly fought. Of his own court-martial he reminisced in bitter and righteous words, placing himself among "a number of brigade and regimental commanders" who were arrested and tried on Buell's orders "presumptively for disorders committed by their troops, but really for the great offense, as it was then considered, of feeding some of those troops upon the resources of the enemy's country."[41] Food supplies of the Union Army were bad, he insisted, and he vowed that he would ten times rather have stood the result of a courtmartial than to have permitted the men to starve.[42]

His former soldiers and other patriotic citizens applauded such statements, but here he was, nearing seventy and growing infirm, with no steady income for himself and his wife. He used his precious violin as a means of livelihood, playing at concerts in the small towns of southern Illinois. "We old fellows are back numbers," he said, "and must not expect too much." He kept silent about his poverty, and the Polish neighbors came to him with food and other help.

He roamed the fields and woods of Radom with his inevitable shotgun and cigarette, and from time to time flared up in fits of anger at the injustices of the world. He had indulged in land speculation which cost him his home, but, when this was foreclosed, the purchaser hesitated to move in, fearing the old man's temper. The buyer finally sold the place to a friend of the General who within a year took possession. Turchin then built a house similar to the first, within a few hundred yards, and with his wife lived there until his end.

Tales of his poverty reached Washington. Senator Joseph B. Foraker of Ohio had been a captain in Turchin's brigade, and General C. H. Grosvenor had also served under the Mad Cossack. Together these two began to agitate for a pension for Turchin, and finally Congress voted $50 per month. But the years and troubles were weighing upon the General. Turchin's mind wavered, and one day he took his entire library out into the yard and built a fire with it. Neighbors tried to save some of the books, but with little success.[43]

[41]*Ibid.*, p. 12.

[42]*The Chicago Tribune*, February 6, 1886.

[43]Turchin's last years are described by me on the basis of the obituaries of June 1901. Most valuable help was also given to me by my friend and colleague of the University of Chicago days, James Monaghan, now of the staff of the Illinois State Historical Library at Springfield, Ill. Some years ago Mr. Monaghan visited Turchin's old home at Radom, photographed his houses, and interviewed his neighbors concerning the General's last days. Generously, Mr. Monaghan has shared with me his notes on those re̶͏̶͏̶

In April, 1901 he was taken to the State Hospital for the Insane, also known as the Southern Illinois Asylum, near Anna, Illinois, where Dr. Samuel Dodds ascribed the General's demented state to the sunstroke suffered on the march through Georgia in 1864. That was surely the foundation of Turchin's illness, said the good doctor patriotically. On the night of June 18, 1901, at the age of seventy-nine, the Mad Cossack of the Grand Army of the Republic died, survived by his wife, mourned by her and their many friends.

His body, draped in an American flag, was brought to the town of Anna and from there, escorted by members of the G.A.R., to the National Soldiers' Cemetery at Mounds City. "A gentleman of the best make," wrote the historian of the old Nineteenth.[44] "Fought for human liberty and for the eternal principle of the right," recalled the writer of an obituary.[45]

And by coincidence, yet as if to show that Russia could ever be expected to send some of her best sons to help America in her fight for, and understanding of, liberty and justice, a few days later—on June 21, to be exact—there arrived in Chicago a Russian professor named Maxim Maximovich Kovalevsky. He came to lecture at the new and fast-growing University of Chicago, and his way and stay were paid by Charles R. Crane—out of the profits Crane was then making by selling Westinghouse air-brakes and other necessary gadgets to the new and fast-growing industries of Russia.

[44]Haynie, *The Nineteenth Illinois*, p. 134.
[45]*The Chicago Record-Herald*, June 20, 1901.

HARVARD UNIVERSITY
RUSSIAN RESEARCH CENTER
1958

The Russian Research Center was officially
opened on February 1, 1948. The following
is a short history of the center covering
a ten year period of activities.

Source: Harvard University, Russian Research Center. Ten-Year Report and Current
Projects. Cambridge, Massachusetts: 1958.

During the spring of 1947 the staff of the Carnegie Corporation inquired into the possibility of a program in the field
of Russian studies which would give some emphasis to research and training in the fields of psychology, sociology, and
anthropology. The previous year had seen two new developments at Harvard, the setting up of a Russian Studies Program
leading to the M.A. degree and the formation of the Department of Social Relations, a department which embraced
clinical and social psychology, social anthropology and sociology. These two factors were influential in the decision of
the Carnegie Corporation to choose Harvard University as
the sponsor for the new Russian program.

Early autumn of 1947 saw consultations between Messrs.
Gardner and Dollard of the Corporation and the Provost and
members of the Harvard Faculty. By the end of October
the University had accepted the invitation of the Corporation to undertake a pilot and planning study, and a director
and executive committee were appointed. Arrangements
were made for the assignment to the Center staff of a portion
of the time of various Harvard scholars specializing in this
area, and two additional appointments were made. A few
graduate student fellows were selected who knew the Russian
language and who were interested in doing theses on
the USSR.

The Center began operations as an organization on February 1, 1948. The initial staff included two full-time research
associates, six faculty members on part time, five graduate
student fellows, an associate director, and a director. The
central task of the first semester was that of surveying existing research in this field, exploring the availability of data,
and determining whether or not a worth-while program for
a longer period could be devised. The staff met weekly as

a group with other members of the Harvard Faculty whose
time had not been formally assigned to the Center. Most
meetings were led off by a visiting scholar from the United
States or Britain who presented his views as to major gaps
in research on the USSR and as to ways and means by which
these gaps could best be filled. A tentative program was
agreed upon, and in May the Carnegie Corporation agreed
to support the work of the Center over a five-year period,
beginning July 1, 1948. Subsequent grants extended the
period of the Corporation's support until 1963.

The early work of the Center staff was necessarily dependent upon the availability of published materials and un-
published manuscripts. Much effort has been devoted, with
excellent collaboration from the Director of the Harvard
University Libraries and his associates, to increasing the University's already rich resources in the Russian field by sub-
scribing to additional contemporary Soviet publications, procuring rare books and pamphlets, and building up a substantial
collection of microfilms of sources not avaiable in print.

The Library of the Russian Research Center itself is
designed to service the needs of researchers for microfilm,
periodical and reference resources. This supplements the
Slavic collection of the Harvard University libraries, which
now contains 65,000 titles, housed mainly in the Widener
Library, the Houghton Library and the Library of the Law
School. Among the collections available in the Houghton
Library is the Trotsky Archive of Trotsky's private papers,
including the Russian Collection (1917–1929) and the International Collection (1929–1940). Houghton Library also
contains the Kilgour Collection of Russian Belles-Lettres and
will soon publish a catalogue of 1,300 first editions from this
collection.

One of the problems still facing serious research in the
Russian field is the lack of opportunity to pursue research
projects in the Soviet Union itself. However, recently re-
strictions on tourist travel to Russia were lifted and since that
date twenty-seven members of our staff and alumni have

been on 30-day tourist visits to the Soviet Union. This has helped to give a feel for the country and its people to re-researchers whose previous knowledge was based entirely upon printed material, but extended research in Russia itself has still not become possible.

Arrangements were made in 1948 for the publication by the Harvard University Press of the Russian Research Center series of books and monographs. Thirty such volumes have appeared and four more are at the Press. In addition to the books, approximately three hundred and fifty articles and chapters in books have been published, of which 59 resulted from the findings of the Harvard Project on the Soviet Social System.

In the period from June 1950 through November 1954, a substantial part of the energies of the Center were devoted to this project, which operated under Contract No. AF 33 (038)–12909 with the Officer Education Research Laboratory, Maxwell Air Force Base, Montgomery, Alabama. Basic data for this study was obtained by a team of twenty interviewers who spent nearly a year in Munich interviewing former Soviet citizens, in order to obtain a more detailed picture of many facets of Soviet life. 336 life history interviews, 375 specialized topical interviews, and more than 1200 written questionnaires were collected in Munich and, in a control study, in New York. From this material fifty major reports were delivered to the Air Force. The principal significance of this investigation was that it made it possible, for the first time, for a group of scholarly researchers from the disciplines of history, economics, politics, sociology, anthropology, and social and clinical psychology, to address themselves to the broad problem of the nature of the Soviet social system. The project, therefore, gave a considerable impetus to this brand of Soviet studies. Much of this material has been published in book and article form (see below, pps. 61–65)

During the year 1953–54 Professor Clyde Kluckhohn, who had been the director of the Center from the beginning, resigned the directorship, and on July 1, 1954 Professor William

L. Langer, Coolidge Professor of History at Harvard, became the new director. In September 1954 Mr. Marshall D. Shulman, formerly with the State Department, was appointed associate director.

In the past decade the Center has awarded graduate student fellowships to fifty-seven individuals. Six of these are currently holding fellowships here and nine are still candidates for the Ph.D. although in many cases teaching elsewhere. Thirty-seven fellows have already received the doctorate. Their doctoral dissertations are not listed as such in this report, but most of them have already been published in book or article form or are being carried forward as current projects. Of these thirty-seven fellows who have received the doctorate, twenty-nine are now teaching, four are in government service, and four hold research positions. Five of our former fellows are no longer working for the doctorate.

One of the marked developments in the character of the Center in recent years has been the increasing use of it by scholars who are supported by funds from other sources and who, as Associates of the Center, contribute to the vitality of its group life. In the year 1957–1958, 22 such Associates from various parts of the United States and abroad carried forward their research work at the Center.

In January 1957 the Committee on Regional Studies was reorganized under the chairmanship of Professor Langer. It now has the general responsibility on policy matters not only for the regional training programs but also for the three research centers located at 16 Dunster Street: The Center for East Asian Studies, the Center for Middle Eastern Studies and the Russian Research Center. As a result, the area program on the Soviet Union, a two-year graduate program leading to the M.A. degree, is more closely associated with the Center.

VLADIMIR NABOKOV
GREAT RUSSIAN AMERICAN WRITER
1969

Vladimir Nabokov, one of the great contemporary literary figures, came to the
United States in 1940, and became a
United States citizen in 1945. The following excerpts reveal interesting facets
of Nabokov's life and writings.

Source: Contemporary Authors. Detroit,
Michigan: Gale Research Company, 1969,
vol. 5-8.

**NABOKOV, Vladimir (Vladimirovich) 1899-
(V. Sirin [until 1940])**

PERSONAL: Name pronounced Vla-*dee*-meer Nah-
boak-off; born April 23, 1899, in St. Petersburg, Russia;
came to United States, 1940; became U.S. citizen, 1945;
son of Vladimir Dmitrievich (a jurist and statesman) and
Elena Ivanovna (Rukavishnikov) Nabokov; married Vera
(Evseevna) Slonim (his amanuensis, aide, chauffeur, and
general helpmate), April 15, 1925; children: Dmitri (a
translator, an operatic bass, and a part-time racing
driver). *Education:* Attended Prince Tenishev School, St.
Petersburg, 1910-17; Trinity College, Cambridge, B.A.
(Romance and Slavic languages), 1922. *Religion:* "Non-
churchgoing Greek Catholic." *Home:* Palace Hotel, Mon-
treux, Switzerland.

CAREER: Left Russia with his family in 1919; lived
in Berlin, Germany, writing, teaching English and tennis,
and composing crossword puzzles (the first such puzzles
in Russian) for the daily emigre newspaper, *Rul,* 1922-37;
lived in Paris, France, 1937-40; Stanford University, Palo
Alto, Calif., instructor in Russian literature and creative
writing, summer, 1941; Wellesley College, Wellesley,
Mass., lecturer in Russian, 1941-48; Harvard University,
Museum of Comparative Zoology, Cambridge, Mass., research fellow in entomology, 1942-48; Cornell University,
Ithaca, N.Y., 1948-59, becoming professor of Russian literature. Visiting lecturer, Harvard University, 1952.
Member: Writers Guild (Los Angeles). *Awards, honors:*
Guggenheim fellowships for creative writing, 1943 and
1952; National Institute of Arts and Letters grant in
literature, 1951; prize for literary achievement from
Brandeis University, 1964.

WRITINGS—Novels: *Mashen'ka* (title means "Mary"),
Slovo (Berlin), 1926; *Korol' Dama Valet,* English translation by Dmitri Nabokov, revised in part by the author,

published as *King, Queen, Knave*, McGraw, 1968; *Zashchita Luzhina*, Slovo, 1930, English translation by Michael Scammell and the author published as "The Luzhin Defense" in *The New Yorker*, May 9 and 16, 1964, and as *The Defense*, Putnam, 1964; *Podvig'* (title means "The Exploit"), Rodnik (Paris), 1932; "Kamera Obskura," published in *Sovremenniya Zapiski* (Paris), 1932, English translation by W. Roy published as *Camera Obscura*, J. Long, 1936, English translation by the author published as *Laughter in the Dark*, Bobbs, 1938; *Otchayanie*, published serially in 1934, published as a book by Petropolis (Berlin), 1936, English translation by the author published as *Despair*, J. Long, 1937, new edition, Putnam, 1966; *Dar*, serialized in *Sovremenniya Zapiski*, 1937, published as a book by Izdatelstvo Imeni Chekhova (New York), 1952, English translation by Dmitri Nabokov and Michael Scammel, in collaboration with the author, published as *The Gift*, Putnam, 1963; *Priglashenie na Kazn'*, Dom Knigi (Paris), 1938, English translation by Dmitri Nabokov, in collaboration with the author, published as *Invitation to a Beheading*, Putnam, 1959; *Soglyadatay*, Russkiya Zapiski (Paris), 1938, English translation by Dmitri Nabokov, in collaboration with the author, serialized in *Playboy* as "The Eye," published in book form as *The Eye*, Phaedra, 1965; "Solus Rex" (unfinished novel), in *Sovremenniya Zapiski*, 1940 (another fragment published in Russian as "Ultima Thule," in *Novy Zhurnal*, New York, 1942); *The Real Life of Sebastian Knight* (first work originally written in English), New Directions, 1941; *Bend Sinister* (first work written in the United States), Holt, 1947; *Lolita*, Olympia Press (Paris), 1955, Putnam, 1958, Russian translation by the author published as *Lolita*, Phaedra, 1966; *Pnin*, Doubleday, 1957; *Pale Fire*, Putnam, 1962; *Ada, or Ardor: A Family Chronicle*, McGraw, 1969.

Stories: *Vozvrashchenie Chorba* (title means "The Return of Chorb"), Slovo, 1929; *Nine Stories*, New Directions, 1947; *Vesna v Fial'te, i Drugie Rasskazy* (title means "Spring in Fialta, and Other Stories"), Izdatelstvo Imeni Chekhova, 1956; *Nabokov's Dozen: A Collection of Thirteen Stories*, Doubleday, 1958, paperback edition published as *Spring in Fialta*, Popular Library, 1960; *Nabokov's Quartet* (four stories, three translated from the Russian by Dmitri Nabokov), Phaedra, 1966.

Autobiography: *Conclusive Evidence: A Memoir*, Harper, 1951, published in England as *Speak, Memory*, Gollancz, 1951, published in Russian as *Drugiye Berega*, Izdatelstvo Imeni Chekhova, 1954, new English-language edition published as *Speak, Memory: An Autobiography Revisited* (Book-of-the-Month Club selection), Putnam, 1966.

Poetry: Privately published a booklet of verse in St. Petersburg, 1914, and a collection of poetry (with V. Balaschov), again in St. Petersburg, 1917; *Grozd'* (title means "The Grape"), Gamayun (Berlin), 1923; *Gorny Put'* (title means "Heavenly Way"), Grani (Berlin), 1923; *Stikhotvoreniya, 1920-1951*, Rifma (Paris), 1952; *Poems*, Doubleday, 1959.

Plays: "Smerti" (verse play; title means "Death"), 1923; "Dedushka" (verse play; title means "The Grandfather"), 1923; "Polius" (verse play; title means "The [North] Pole"), 1924; "Tragedia gospodina Morna" (title means "The Tragedy of Mr. Morn"), 1924-25(?); "Tshelovek in SSSR" (five-act play; title means "The Man from the U.S.S.R."), 1927 (only act one has been published); "Sobytie" (three-act comedy; title means "The Event"; performed in Paris, 1938, in New York, 1941), published in *Russkiya Zapiski*, 1938; "Izobretenie Val'sa" (three-act

play), published in *Russkiya Zapiski*, 1938, English trans-
lation by Dmitri Nabokov and the author published as
The Waltz Invention, Phaedra, 1966, first produced by
Hartford Stage Company, Hartford, Conn., January, 1969.

Other prose: *Nikolai Gogol*, New Directions, 1944; (author
of introduction and notes) Mikhail Lermontov, *Hero in
Our Time*, translation by Dmitri Nabokov, Doubleday,
1958; *Notes on Prosody* (from the commentary to his
translation of Pushkin's *Eugene Onegin*), Pantheon,
1965; *Nabokov's Congeries* (reader), edited by Page Steg-
ner, Viking, 1968.

Translator into English: (With Edmund Wilson) Pushkin,
"Mozart and Salieri," in *New Republic*, April 21, 1941;
*Three Russian Poets: Selections from Pushkin, Lermon-
tov, and Tyutchev*, New Directions, 1945; (from Old
Russian, with introduction and commentary) *The Song of
Igor's Campaign: An Epic of the Twelfth Century*,
Vintage, 1960; (and editor and author of commentary)
Alexander Pushkin, *Eugene Onegin*, four volumes, Panthe-
on, 1964.

Translator into Russian: (From the French) Romain
Rolland, *Nikolka Persik* (French title: *Colas Breugnon*),
Slovo, 1922; (from the English) Lewis Carroll, *Anya v
Strane Chudes* (English title: *Alice in Wonderland*),
Gamayun (Berlin), 1923.

Contributor to Russian emigre journals in Berlin, Paris,
and New York, and to *New Yorker, Atlantic, Harper's,
Partisan Review, Hudson Review, Reporter, Esquire* and
other publications; contributor of papers on lepidoptera to
such scientific journals as the *Bulletin* of the Museum of
Comparative Zoology, Harvard, one such paper bearing
the title "The Nearctic Members of the Genus *Lycaeides*
Huebner." Wrote screenplay for "Lolita," produced by
Metro-Goldwyn-Mayer, 1962, in a somewhat altered
form.

WORK IN PROGRESS: A novel, *The Texture of Time*; a
number of essays on several works, including those of
James Joyce and Franz Kafka; a collection of his papers
on lepidopterology; plans to publish the complete and
original screenplay that he wrote for "Lolita"; the second
installment of his autobiography, *Speak on, Memory*.

SIDELIGHTS: Nabokov, a White Russian immigrant to
the United States, who came via Cambridge and the
Continent, has come to be regarded by many as the
foremost stylist and experimenter currently writing in
English. "Without attempting to deal with Nabokov,"
writes E. Rubinstein, "we cannot expect to understand the
literary culture of today as distinguished from that of a
generation ago." Anthony Burgess considers *Pale Fire* to
be "the first major formal innovation in the novel since
Finnegans Wake. ... It is the one book of the post-Joyce
era that most novelists would give their eyeteeth not just
to have written but to start writing: the magician's joy
confronts us on the first page." A more reserved admirer,
Stephen Koch, writes: "Despite his great verbal gifts, his
merely conventionally excellent works immediately reveal
their trivial, antiquated forms. ... Nabokov's is a virtu-
oso, rather than original, genius." Koch adds, however,
that Nabokov's "wit and the stunning ingenuity of his
formal devices (particularly in *Pale Fire*) easily surpass
those of any other novelist now writing in English." And
Geoffrey Wolff says that "it's really insufferably monoto-
nous to open book after book by this man and discover
him incapable of composing a dull book, of writing a
graceless sentence or using an inappropriate word. Hasn't
he ever thought a stupid thought?"

Although Nabokov originally wrote in Russian, starting with poems at the age of thirteen, he had learned to read English before he could read Russian. Later he learned French (the quantity of his pieces written in French is very slight), and became as he recalls "a perfectly normal trilingual child." In his evocative autobiography he recounts what he claims to be his ancestry, from the first caveman who painted a medieval Tartar prince, down to his father, a liberal statesman who participated in the 1917 revolution and was assassinated by a Russian fascist at a Berlin lecture in 1922. Also among his forebears were German barons, a lesser Decembrist, an obscure Crusader, and an eighteenth-century German composer. After the revolution Nabokov lost the two million dollar fortune he had inherited and his country estate, becoming a permanent wanderer who has never again owned his own home. Temporarily his residence is Switzerland; "home" is America, "it is my country," he says. "The intellectual life suits me better there than any other country in the world. I have more friends there, more kindred souls than anywhere." Though he has been invited to visit the Soviet Union, he has never done so.

Thousands of pages of criticism have sought to explicate Nabokov's work. Nabokov finds this criticism most instructive "when an expert proves to me that my facts or my grammar are wrong." In the foreword to the Time-Life edition of *Bend Sinister* he discounts as useless many of the attempts to categorize him and his books. He writes: "I have never been interested in what is called the literature of social comment (in journalistic and commercial parlance: 'great books'). I am not 'sincere,' I am not 'provocative,' I am not 'satirical.' I am neither a didacticist nor an allegorizer. Politics and economics, atomic bombs, primitive and abstract art forms, the entire Orient, symptoms of 'thaw' in Soviet Russia, the Future of Mankind, and so on, leave me supremely indifferent." Another time he wrote: "For me the work of fiction exists only in so far as it affords me what I shall bluntly call aesthetic bliss; that is, a sense of being somehow, somewhere, connected with other states of being where art (curiosity, tenderness, kindness, ecstasy) is the norm."

His aesthetic bliss is achieved by conceiving of art as artifice. Patricia Merivale notes how he "never lets his readers forget that he is the conjuror, the illusionist, the stage-manager, to whom his characters owe their existence." A Nabokov narrator is what Nabokov terms "an anthropomorphic deity impersonated by me." His characters are men of imagination, cast as near-freaks in their society. John O. Lyons describes Nabokov's favorite narrative method as "the examination of a text (or vision of aesthetic order) by some real or imagined artist who vies with God in disordering a universe. This explains his fervor in defense of his own literary Olympians: Shakespeare, Pope, Sterne, Byron, Pushkin, Gogol, and Joyce, and why he expresses an unbounded contempt for certain literary heretics like Dostoyevsky and Mann." Though art at its greatest is for Nabokov "fantastically deceitful and complex," it at the same time "contains far more intrinsical truths than life's reality." Nabokov has what Clarence Brown calls "a very Tolstoyan passion for the truth."

As a master of language Nabokov has few peers. He "handles our language as if he had invented it," writes Julian Moynahan, "and he is constantly inventive with respect to narrative form." In truth, he did invent a portion of our language, the word "nymphet" and other variations on established words, as well as "krestoslovitsa," the Russian word for crossword puzzles. Alan

Pryce-Jones notes that Nabokov at times "is making a
language from scratch, with all the intoxication of a
magician who finds himself to be even more capable than
he dared hope. . . . He can be watched, like a potter,
shaping the language as he goes, digging up an obsolete
word, pillaging the dictionary for possible but untried
usages." He enjoys sending his readers to an unabridged
lexicon. Furthermore, the obscurity of certain passages is
increased because he is careful to not endow his words with
too much "verbal body": "We think not in words but in
shadows of words," he says. And his fondness for word
play might be likened to that of his protagonist in *Despair*
who says: "I liked, as I like still, to make words look
self-conscious and foolish, to bind them by the mock
marriage of a pun, to turn them inside out, to come upon
them unawares. What is this jest in majesty? This ass in
passion? How do God and Devil combine to form a live
dog?" Despite all the plaudits that his masterful sentences
have received, Nabokov maintains what can only be called
a false modesty. He recently wrote: "My private tragedy
. . . is that I had to abandon my natural idiom, my
untrammelled, rich and infinitely docile Russian tongue
for a second-rate brand of English. . . ."
Nabokov's life was relatively quiet, the life of a Cornell
professor lecturing to "the great fraternity of C-minus,
backbone of the nation," and, he says, loving it, when
Lolita, a book begun in 1939 or 1940 during "a severe
attack of intercostal neuralgia," was published in Paris.
For his protection he was hidden away by his publisher.
The book was denounced in the House of Commons and
banned in several countries, including France. The *Chicago
Tribune* refused to review it. "No," Nabokov told *Playboy,* "I shall never regret *Lolita.* She was like the
composition of a beautiful puzzle." Another time he said:
"What bothered me most was the belief that *Lolita* was a
criticism of America. I think that's ridiculous. I don't see
how anybody could find it in *Lolita.* I don't like people
who see the book as an erotic phenomenon, either. Even
more, I suppose, I don't like people who have not read
Lolita and think it obscene. . . . I don't think *Lolita* is a
religious book, but I do think it is a moral one." Harry T.
Moore compares this novel to *Candide,* and *Lolita* has
indeed become a classic tale. Nabokov says that among his
books it holds first place in his affections. (Elsewhere,
however, he has said of *King, Queen, Knave:* "Of all my
novels this bright brute is the gayest.")
He has never learned to type. He tells his interviewers:
"In my twenties and early thirties, I used to write, dipping
pen in ink and using a new nib every other day in
exercise books, crossing out, inserting, striking out again,
crumpling the page, rewriting every page three or four
times, then copying out the novel in a different ink and a
neater hand, then revising the whole thing once more,
re-copying it with new corrections, and finally dictating it
to my wife who has typed out all my stuff. Generally
speaking I am a slow writer, a snail carrying its house at
the rate of two hundred pages of final copy per year (one
spectacular exception was the Russian original of *Invitation to a Beheading,* the first draft of which I wrote in one
fortnight of wonderful excitement and sustained inspira-
tion). . . . I relied heavily on mental composition, con-
structing whole paragraphs in my mind as I walked in the
streets or sat in my bath, or lay in bed, although often
deleting or rewriting them later. In the late 'thirties,
beginning with *The Gift,* and perhaps under the influence
of the many notes needed, I switched to another, physically more practical, method—that of writing with an
eraser-capped pencil on index cards." He still writes on

index cards, revises the cards many times, and dictates the finished novel to his wife. He admits he needs readers (an ideal reader would be "a little Nabokov"), but adds: "In the long run, . . . it is only the author's private satisfaction that counts."

In addition to authors already mentioned in this connection, Nabokov dislikes William Faulkner, the Beats, Angry Young Men, Existentialists, Joseph Conrad, Tolstoy, Pasternak,—and Hemingway, on whom he's been quoted thus: "I read a novel of his in 1940. I can't quite remember the title. ... *Bulls? Bells? Balls?*" He also has no use for detective or historical novels. Among contemporaries, he says, "I do have a few favorites—for example, Robbe-Grillet and Borges." He has said he likes Melville and Hawthorne. The only literary influence he will admit to is Pierre Delalande, whom, he adds impishly, he himself invented. He belongs to no "school" of writing and has in fact said that "there is only one school: that of talent."

Chess became his "queer substitute" for music, which he has no ear for. Chess, which frequently enters his novels, sometimes, as in *The Defense*, playing a major role, he explains thus: "It should be understood that competition in chess problems is not really between White and Black but between the composer and the hypothetical solver (just as in a first-rate work of fiction the real clash is not between the characters but between the author and the world), so that a great part of the problem's value is due to the number of 'tries'—delusive opening moves, false scents, specious lines of play, astutely and lovingly prepared to lead the would-be solver astray."

He is much more than an amateur lepidopterist, having discovered and named several new species and sub-species (one, "Nabokov's wood nymph"). Perhaps he inherited this interest from his father whom he once recalls as a participant in the pursuit and netting of a rare butterfly on August 17, 1883. Gold writes: "He has a passion for butterflies and spends long periods chasing up hill and down dale with net and wife." Nabokov admits that this "passion for lepidopterological research, in the field, in the laboratory, in the library, is even more pleasurable than the study and practice of literature, which is saying a good deal." His two passions do not conflict, however, because he realizes that "there is no science without fancy, and no art without facts."

Laughter in the Dark, screenplay by Edward Bond, has been filmed by Woodfall Films, 1969; *Ada, or Ardor* has been bought by Columbia; Wolper Pictures purchased film rights to *King, Queen, Knave* in 1968; *Invitation to a Beheading* was dramatized by Russell Mc-Grath and performed in New York for the Shakespeare Festival, at the New York Public Theatre, March 8-May 4, 1969.

A RUSSIAN AMERICAN COMMUNITY
IN NEW JERSEY
1969

On a trip in the state of New Jersey, Len
and Jean Gashel "discovered" and described
New Kuban, a small community of Russian
Cossaks who came and settled in the United
States in 1918.

Source: Travel, vol. 131 (June 1969).

The next stop is the Cossack community of New Kuban where you will enter the Pine Barrens proper. In about ten miles south of Glassboro, turn left onto U.S. Route 40 heading east to Buena. In twelve miles turn left onto Route 54 in the center of Buena. Watch for a Sunoco service station on the right after two miles. Turn right at the next intersection onto the black-topped Weymouth Road. It is just over a mile to the Cossack Community.

The first clue that you have reached New Kuban is a series of roadside mail boxes on the right with distinctly Russian names, such as Ponochovny, Nazarova, Galkin and Polupanow. There are no stores, offices or other outward signs of community life. The 50 some houses in the village are obscured behind rows of oak trees bordering Weymouth Road.

The residents are mostly elderly and speak only Russian. Many are camera shy. Women wearing babushkas are often seen working in small gardens around their houses.

As Cossacks, these people were designated by Russia's czars to defend the country's borders. Some of the residents of New Kuban fought with the White Army supporting Czar Nicholas II against the Com-

munist Red Army. They were forced to flee Russia with the downfall of the monarchy in 1918. Most of the residents of New Kuban remain intensely loyal to the long-lost Czarist tradition.

At the first road intersection in New Kuban look for a small sign pointing to a monastery. Turn right onto a gravel road and in a block turn left to a dead end. The last building is the one-man monastery of Father Adam.

Father Adam welcomes visitors graciously despite the fact that he speaks only Russian. If you are lucky, an interpreter from the neighborhood will happen along to help you overcome the language barrier. But in any event, don't miss the opportunity to visit the monastery and meet Father Adam. With his long white beard and flowing black robe, he looks the role of a Russian religious leader from the Czarist era.

The monastery is a red and grey stone building surmounted by a pink siding roof. It is open every day during daylight hours. Discarded cat food cans serve as candle holders in the basement chapel of the building beneath the main sanctuary. They are not as out-of-place in the overall setting as might be imagined. Paintings on the walls of the chapel are the work of two Greenwich Village artists who worked without pay.

After leaving the monastery, retrace your route back to Weymouth Road. Turn right and proceed about half a mile to the Russian Orthodox Church on the left. This is the real landmark of the community. It is a white concrete building with a green roof topped by a Slavic bulb-shaped spire. A gold Russian cross with an angled bar below the cross bar and a smaller cross bar on top rises above the church.

A large Russian cross stands on a knoll behind the church about a hundred yards down a narrow tree-lined lane. On the way you will pass the church cemetery. Notice the head stones with inscriptions in Russian and pictures of the deceased.

The best time to visit the Russian Church is Sunday morning for the two to three-hour service which begins about 9:00 a.m. You will be encouraged by members of the congregation to take a seat on the back benches. A word of advice—accept the offer. The congregation, including the most elderly, remain standing throughout the entire service and it can be very tiring for someone unaccustomed to this.

The service is entirely in Russian but is colorful enough to hold a visitor's attention. To see the chapel lit by candlelight and to listen to the moving Russian music is a memorable experience. Notice particularly a small box on the church altar. It contains soil from Russia brought over by the refugees and is one of the most prized possessions of the community.

THE TOLSTOY FOUNDATION CENTER
1972

The Tolstoy Foundation Center, formerly
known as the Reed Farm, located twenty
miles outside New York City, presents a
record of original activities related to
the process of resettling tens of thousands of Russian and other ethnic groups
of immigrants.

Source: Tolstoy Foundation Inc. Thirty-
Four Years of Assistance to Refugees. New
York: 1972.

The position of the Tolstoy Foundation in the United
States was stabilized by a generous anonymous gift
through the Commonwealth Foundation in 1941. This
was the Reed Farm — 75 acres of land five miles north
of Nyack, in Rockland County, N.Y. It included a barn,
sheds, and some buildings used as a rest home. Over
the years it became an initial haven and resettlement
center for over 6,500 Displaced Persons of World War II.
This represents roughly one third of some 23,000
persons brought over to the United States and directly
sponsored by TF under special Congressional legisla-
tion in behalf of refugees scattered all over the world
after World War II.
The name "Reed Farm" was something of a mis-
nomer, as its prime function after 1945 was to serve as
a center of resettlement and integration. From the out-
set, the straight farming activities (chicken farm with
5,000 birds, thoroughbred hogs, cattle, and some 12
acres of truck gardening) were to serve as occupational
therapy for assimilation of newcomers to this country
and for aged and physically handicapped persons. The
efforts of management were concentrated on various
cultural aspects of the best of Russian life and culture.
With this main purpose in mind, there was established
a year-round camp for some 20 needy children. Up until
1959, there were 80–90 children there during two summer months. Lectures in Russian and in English were
organized for student groups of the Federated Russian
Orthodox Clubs of North America and to the present
time Reed Farm is used for religious retreats of Russian Orthodox Sunday School teachers and for students
of the various Orthodox Theological Seminaries and
Academies.
The original Home Chapel, dedicated in 1940, later,
after small damage caused by a fire in 1950, was trans-

ferred to the basement of a two-story building which
had been erected in 1949 for the temporary housing of
incoming refugees. A permanent Church built in the
classic Pskov-Novgorod style and dedicated to St.
Sergius of Radonezh was erected in 1957, exclusively
from the contributions of its congregation, which is
still paying for the completion of its inner decoration.

Additionally — following many readjustments of emphasis in order to keep abreast of changing conditions
— the Center now offers many public services other
than those originally conceived. Successfully operating
are a Home for the Aged (some 45 residents), a library
of some 27,000 volumes, a central administrative office
and guest accommodations with dining and recreational
facilities, including a swimming pool.

A Nursing Home with 96 beds on the premises of the
Tolstoy Foundation Center was built with New York
State funds and was opened on September 11, 1970, and
is operating under full occupancy.

St. Sergius Church, built in 1957, presents many features of interest in the field of Russian Church Art. A
resident priest contributes to the spiritual atmosphere
of the varied population of this resettlement and cultural Center.

A large storage of gift clothing, which is cleaned,
sorted, and packaged, provides shipments to indigents
throughout the world.

Seminars for students are conducted both during winter and summer sessions.

General farming (5,000 chickens, pigs, Angus cattle,
a vegetable garden) complements the total Center complex and favorably affects the quality and the cost of
food.

RUSSIAN BUILDINGS AND PLACES IN SITKA, ALASKA
1972

> The Cathedral of Archangel St. Michael in
> Sitka, Alaska, and the Sitka National Histori-
> cal Park have an interesting history going back
> to the beginning of the nineteenth century. Here
> is their brief history, and their present day con-
> dition.

Source: Sitka Troika, January-March 1972.

THE CATHEDRAL OF ARCHANGEL ST. MICHAEL

Czarist Russia first sent exploring parties across the Bering Sea in 1741 when Vitus Bering sighted the Aleutian Chain and recognized the fact that he had discovered virgin territory.

Succeeding Russian expeditions sailed to this new land with varying success. As the size of the Russian Colonies grew at Kodiak, so did the influence of the Russian Orthodox faith, for with each expedition one or two priests were required to sail to the missionary field to convert natives to Christianity. The missionaries endured great hardships.

The Church gained momentum when Alexander Baranof, a hard-working and a controversial person, took over the management of the Russian Colonies in 1790. While Baranof had strong feelings about the natives becoming Christians, his own drinking and his boisterous social life outraged the priests. He, in turn, regarded the clergy as drones and non-producers. It was not a happy relationship. The Church continued to expand and in mid-1800's its influence spread over the endless miles of the Alaskan shores from the Arctic through the Aleutian chain, throughout the Panhandle to the Bay Area of California.

In 1842, the Russian-American Company's Charter was renewed with a stipulation made by the Czarist Government that the Company should support the Church's missionary work throughout the colonies; and that they should construct an imposing cathedral in Sitka. Sitka, by this time, developed into a wilderness metropolis and its fame spread among the trading fleets of the world. Under the able management of Governor Etolin, Finnish woodworkers constructed during 1844-1848, in the heart of Sitka, the beautiful Cathedral of St. Michael. The Cathedral was a magnificent spiritual landmark as well as a geographic landmark for over a hundred years until it, along with the center of the Sitka business district, was destroyed by the devastating fire of January 2, 1966.

The Church was built of logs and handhewn planks, in the form of a cross, and included three chapels--on the far right, the Chapel of St. John the Baptist; in the center, the main Chapel of St. Michael; and on the left, the Chapel of Our Lady of Kazan of which the "Sitka Madonna" icon is representative. Other notable treasures of the old church were the iconstas or screens between the main chapel and the chapel of Saint Michael. The screens contained the "Royal Doors" on which the icons were reputedly decorated with about fifty pounds of silver. All of the valuable icons and furniture of the church were saved from destruction except the icon of the "Lord's Supper" which was fastened securely above the Royal Doors. This prevented the removal of the icon in spite of the heroic efforts of Sitka citizens. The valuable relics will be rehoused in the new replica of St. Michael's.

The reconstruction of the cathedral began in July 1967. In the initial fund drive, early that year, about $260,000 was raised so the construction work was placed on bids. The bids presented by three contractors were extremely high, far above the amount of money on hand for the purpose. After much negotiation and decision making, plans were made to proceed with the basement phase. C & R Builders contracted to excavate and construct a foundation to meet the U.S. Corps of Engineers' specifications for prime earthquake zones. Heating and plumbing was included which gave the parishioners a place to worship and to store salvaged valuables. The completion of this phase left a balance of $82,500 in the bank which accumulated interest for three years. In 1970, Leslie Yaw, a retired longtime Sitka businessman, initiated and started a new fund drive to raise $100,000 in Alaska with same amount to be matched by the Seattle area; $250,000 to be raised by mortgaging property of the Russian Orthodox Church--Alaska Diocese; and $50,000 from other sources. It was hoped that this total of $500,000 would finish the project even with the ten-percent increase in costs of construction over the dormant period.

Alaskans raised their portion of the budget but the Sitka business community made up a large proportion of the donations. The Seattle area then undergoing an economic depression was far below expectations. Also at the time of signing the mortgage early in 1972, the Alaskan Orthodox Diocese had a complete turnover of its top clergy so there was a delay in the construction work through most of 1972, until the new administrator could check details. After many conferences with Architect Sergey Padukow and Shupp Construction of Sitka, the unfinished work was divided into phases, each phase was to be paid for as soon as it was completed. The complete concrete inner shell of the structure was built, the steel bell tower was erected and enclosed with fireproof planking; all roofs were installed and sealed including the great dome which was covered with copper. To crown the efforts, the steeple and the onion-shaped cupolas, with their crosses, were received from the East a few days before the Alaska Day celebration, October 18, 1972. The steeple and cupolas were installed under the supervision of the architect during the Alaska Day festivities. All bills are paid and a balance of $30,000 is left in the treasury. Archpriest Father Joseph Kreta, the new administrator for the Orthodox Church in Alaska, has pledged his complete cooperation toward raising funds and completing the Cathedral. Joe Ashby, a twenty-five-year resident of Sitka and one of its most ardent history buffs, is chairman of the Sitka Historical Sites Restoration Committee and states that he is confident that by this time next year the reconstruction of St. Michael's will be completed.

SITKA NATIONAL HISTORICAL PARK

Sitka Additions

One of the contributors to the "Sitka Troika" has been Sitka National Monument. Sitka National Monument is no more. By an act of Congress that was signed into law on October 18, 1972, the name was changed to Sitka National Historical Park, a name that is commensurate with the historical significance of the Park.

Through this law, the National Park Service is authorized to acquire and add some 53 acres to the existing park. Of these, 49 are tidelands that played an important part in the Park story. It was across these tidelands that the Russians attacked the Tlingit fort in 1804. Here also, Katlian, the Tlingit battle leader, wearing his raven hat and armed with only a blacksmith's hammer, singlehandedly threw the Russians into confusion by his surprise flank attack.

Along with the historic tidelands, the National Park Service is authorized to acquire the Russian Mission in Sitka, which was in continuous use until 1969. This structure is one of the oldest and most significant Russian buildings in the state. Built in 1842 by Bishop Innocent Veniaminof, it served as a residence for the Orthodox clergy, as a school for the children of the Russian-American Company, and as a seminary for the Orthodox Church.

The Park Service plans call for the purchase and the complete restoration of the Russian Mission. When the project is completed, the building will be open to the public. Among the interpretive possibilities of the Russian Mission are, of course, the significance of the building itself, the Russian settlement of Sitka, and the influence of the Orthodox Church. It is impossible at this time to give project dates because the plans are dependent upon the availability of appropriated funds.

Impetus for the project began with a Park Service study in 1968. However, it was the support and the aggressive determination of Senators Stevens and Gravel and Representative Nick Begich that caused the passage of the Sitka Additions bill by Congress. President Nixon's signature on the bill, on Alaska Day, opened the door to preservation of these historic properties.

THE SITKA 9th INFANTRY

The Sitka 9th Infantry is a recently formed organization of fifteen local men interested in the preservation and accuracy of Sitka's rich historical heritage. On November 13, 1972, the name, Sitka 9th Infantry, was adopted by the organization in order to pattern the unit after the original Company F of the U.S. Army's 9th Infantry which was present at the flag-raising ceremony on October 18, 1867. Company F stayed to serve as Sitka's only permanently stationed military unit. The 9th Infantry, presently based

at Fort Wainwright in Fairbanks, annually visits Sitka on Alaska Day and
has indicated its approval and cooperation with our efforts.

The objective of the Sitka 9th Infantry is to provide Sitka with an au-
thentic 1867 military unit, the only one of its kind in Alaska. The unit will
participate in the Alaska Day parade and ceremonies and will fire cannon
and musket salutes as has been done originally. It intends to act in other
capacities to make Sitka's Alaska Day celebrations as historically accurate
and interesting as possible. Much research has been done concerning the
history of the Russian-American experiences in Alaska and the U.S. military era in Sitka. The results of this research has been incorporated into
the formation of this organization.

In addition to the Alaska Day Activities, the unit plans to take part in
the Fourth of July celebration and other special ceremonies held in Sitka.
It hopes to become a crack drill team representing Sitka as uniquely as is
currently being done by the New Archangel Dancers. It also plans to restore
and maintain the many fine cannons in the area and its scope of activity remains unlimited. The unit will accept suggestions as to how and in what
ways it may become of service to the community.

As a show of good faith, each member of the Sitka 9th Infantry is required to purchase his own musket (approximately $100) which will be an
accurate replica of a weapon issued to the U.S. Army during the American
Civil War.

The Alaska Day Committee expressed its pleasure at the formation
of the unit and pledged $1,000 toward the purchase of uniforms which cost
about $250. each. These will be authentic copies of the dress uniform worn
by men in the U.S. 9th Infantry on October 18, 1867, which consisted of hat,
coat, trousers, boots, belts, cartridge pouches, and insignias. The uniforms
will be purchased through the National Park Service in order to insure au-
thenticity of each minute detail of the uniform.

On October 18, 1867, a 21-gun salute boomed over Sitka Harbor as the
Stars and Stripes was raised over the newly acquired territory of Alaska.
On October 18, 1972, a cannon volley (the first one in over 100 years), fired
by the founders of the Sitka 9th Infantry, once again boomed from Castle Hill
over Sitka Harbor. It is the hope of the newly organized unit that with the
aid and support of the community, it can make the next Alaska Day as memorable as that day, long ago, when the Old Flory was unfurled in an Alaskan
breeze for the first time.

Nathaniel Mandel, Sergeant
Daniel R. Kuehn, Sergeant Major
Brent Scott, Sergeant At Arms

NIKOLAEVSK, A NEW RUSSIAN VILLAGE
IN ALASKA
1972

In 1967 about two hundred Russian Old
Believers purchased land in the Alaskan
wilderness and established a new Alaska
in order to preserve their old customs,
and to shield their children from what
they felt were corrupting influences:
television, tobacco, and drugs. J. Rearden
visited the new village, and shared his
views in a very informative article from
which we have extracted relevant pages.

Source: National Geographic, vol. 142,
no. 3 (September 1972).

IN 1967 four full-bearded Russian expatriates arrived on
the Kenai, seeking land for their people and information on Alaskan living. They had come from an Old
Believer colony in Oregon, looking for a way to escape the
temptations and distractions of modern America, which had
begun to impinge on their lives there. The four inspected
and bought a square mile of wilderness from the state.

"They walked every foot of that section," a farmer who
accompanied them told me. "They found the springs, the
best places to build, and located the best timber."

The first four houses were built in 1968—lonely, raw
cabins in a vast spruce forest. Electricity was brought in by
the local cooperative, and more families arrived.

I live in Homer, on the north shore of Kachemak Bay,
only 25 miles by road from Nikolaevsk, and I flew over the
village in small planes many times during its first years.
I could always tell when a family had arrived from Oregon
—there would be a pile of household goods on the ground,
and nearby, another cabin under construction.

I had serious doubts that the settlement would succeed;
in the 16 years I have lived on the Kenai two earlier attempts at colonization by other groups had failed. But time
has proved the Old Believers knew how to tame a wilderness. Their village is now home to some 200.

The men work in nearby communities, and some have become commercial fishermen. The villagers do not farm for
profit in the short Alaskan summers, but some families
have greenhouses where they grow their own vegetables
(pages 410-11), and a few have outside gardens. Each man
builds his home and supports his family, but, in true pio-

neering and Christian spirit, all work together, too.

"We help each other by trading work," Kiril Martushev, one of the first to arrive, told me.

"And we all built the church together," Kondraty Fefelov, a church elder, said. "But there weren't many of us at Nikolaevsk then. Now we must make it bigger. Maybe we'll finish it after fishing season—if we have a good season."

Villagers must earn money, to complete not only the church but also their own homes. Winter jobs are scarce, so the money earned during the short Alaskan summer must stretch through the long winter.

Salmon fishing has brought little money. Alaska's salmon fisheries are crowded, and competition is keen at nearby Cook Inlet, where only two fishing days a week are allowed during a one-month season. Halibut fishing has been better.

"We made between $400 and $500 every four or five days one June," Ivan Fefelov told me, jubilantly. He and his son-in-law, Vladimir Martushev, fish the boat *Baikal,* which they built together.

Of the 12 top-quality commercial fishing boats now owned by Old Believers, villagers built ten themselves. Eighteen of the men had worked in a furniture factory in Oregon and are experts with wood. Two years after their arrival in Nikolaevsk, several of the men spent the winter building a 32-foot diesel-powered commercial fishing boat in the local sawmill of the Polushkin brothers. Others, like Victor Yakunin and Feodor Basargin, sharpened their skills working in a boat shop 12 miles from Nikolaevsk.

Last winter 15 Old Believers formed the Russian Marine Company, built a shop in Nikolaevsk where five men work, and prepared to produce for sale fiberglass boats of 12-, 16-, and 34-foot lengths. By early spring two 34-foot hulls had come from their largest mold, and one of these was within weeks of launching as a commercial fishing boat to be used by Prohor Martushev. The other hull will be similarly outfitted for Larion Polushkin.

EASTER SUNDAY and the six days following are Nikolaevsk's most important holidays, but I found I would have to march to a different tune if I was to attend at the proper time. The Old Believers determine the dates of holy days not by the Gregorian but by the Julian calendar. December 25, for instance, falls on what is January 7 to all but a few Americans.

The day before Old Believer Easter, I visited the home of 25-year-old Feodor Basargin. He is "Fred" to his *Amerikansky* neighbors, and he is venturing into the construction contracting business. (Shortly after Easter, Fred was elected *starosta,* or mayor, of Nikolaevsk for a one-year term. The ballot was secret, and only the men voted.)

Feodor's married sister Agripena and her husband, Anany Kozhin, were there, as was Victor Yakunin. The three Basargin children, Ulita, Grigory, and Varsanofy, and the two Kozhin children, Alexey and Tatiana, were playing inside the house. The men visited and watched the children, while the women boiled and dyed Easter eggs in the kitchen.

"They're hurrying to get done before church," Feodor explained. The service was to start at four that afternoon.

Between boiling and dyeing eggs, Irina, Feodor's wife, removed rising dough from a wooden tub, punched it down, rolled it, and plunked it into pans to rise on a nearby table.

Not wanting to make the women late for church, I decided to get out of their way, and so walked to the home of Anisim Kalugin. He was one of the four-man advance party that bought the land for Nikolaevsk. During summers he works in a salmon cannery, 45 miles away at Kasilof, and the rest of the year he picks up odd jobs elsewhere. The Kalugin house is one of the largest in Nikolaevsk, with three bedrooms, a big living room, and kitchen. Like the majority of homes, it is heated by firewood; the village has only a few oil stoves. The house was sparkling clean and bright with freshly embroidered cloths on the walls. The eggs were all dyed, and the seven Kalugin children were preparing to go outside to the wood-heated *banya,* or steam bath.

Anisim's wife, Solomia, came through the living room with her hair falling in a great cloud to her waist. The women never cut their hair, and in public they keep it in braids and covered with a *platok,* or head scarf. An unmarried girl wears one braid, but when she marries, which may be as young as 15, her hair is plaited into two braids at the wedding ceremony and worn that way thenceforth.

I chatted with Anisim, and then moved on. As I left, Solomia came out of the banya, wading through the snow and holding 10-month-old towel-wrapped Karnily on her hip. Only his bare feet and head were visible, and they were glowing red from the steam bath.

Until Saturday midnight, Easter services were informal, with elders reading passages from the Bible. The formal services started at midnight, with hallowed rituals that continued until seven in the morning. These rites date back in some respects to those of imperial Byzantium in the eighth century A.D.

THE OLD BELIEVERS cherish that future. I visited the two one-room schoolhouses they persuaded the Kenai Peninsula Borough to build and support. There the youngsters of Nikolaevsk are educated in English. In one room George Wolansky teaches kindergarten and first and second grades. He is a graduate of Western Washington State College, with degrees in Russian and education, and this is his first assignment in Alaska. He lives nine miles away, at Anchor Point, with his wife and 5-year-old son. With the other teacher, Robert Moore, he usually walks two miles from the main road to the school.

Tatiana Martushev, 21, who has four children of her own, works as Wolansky's aide. Using a life-size diagram of a woman in an apron and ankle-length skirt, and with labels in English, she points, and the sweet high voices chant, "Stomach, knee, apron, eyes...." When a child doesn't understand an English word, Tatiana or Wolansky explains in Russian. By third grade most of the children speak English, but not without a Russian accent, since English is spoken only in the classroom.

In the other schoolroom, Robert Moore, who also lives at Anchor Point with his wife and two young daughters, teaches grades three through eight. He had taught for a year at another Kenai Peninsula school. Educated in Tennessee, he claims, facetiously, that he is infusing the Nikolaevsk children with a Southern accent. He does not speak Russian, but he has help from aide Glikeria Kuzmin (page 423).

"I am trying to prepare these children to be productive in an English-speaking society," Moore told me. "The children sometimes struggle with language arts, but they are amazing in mathematics. One 6-year-old can easily add five-digit numbers, five deep, and a seventh-grader does high-school-senior math."

RUSSIAN AMERICANS SUPPORT VIETNAMESE REFUGEES
1975

In one of its editorials, the newspaper
<u>Novoye</u> <u>Russkoye</u> <u>Slovo</u> showed its support
for President Ford's plan of resettling
about 130,000 South Vietnamese refugees.
It also urged Russian Americans to sign
a petition of support and send it to President Ford. The following is the text
of the petition.

Source: <u>Novoye</u> <u>Russkoye</u> <u>Slovo</u>, May 8, 1975.

May......1975

The President Gerald R. Ford
White House
Washington, D. C. 20500

Dear Mr. President:

As an American citizen of Russian descent I
whole-heartedly support your humanitarian policy towards the Vietnam refugees.
I do hope that the Congress will allow the necessary funds for their resettlement in the United
States.

Respectfully yours

....
....
Signature:

....
....
....
Address:

RUSSIAN AMERICANS
AND ALEXANDER SOLZHENITZYN
1975

During the summer of 1975, Alexander
Solzhenitzyn, world famous Russian
exilee writer and Nobel Prize winner,
made a trip to the United States. The
Congress of Russian Americans urged all
Russian Americans to sign petitions and
support a bill authorizing President
Gerald Ford to decalre Alexander Solzhenitzyn
an honorary United States citizen. The
following is the text of the petitions.

Source: <u>Novoye Russkoye Slovo</u>, May 13,
1975.

Honorable_____   (Full Name)

House of Representatives
Washingon, D. C. 20515
   Dear Sir (Madam)
   As your constituent, I respectfully request that you vote in
favor of granting an honorary citizenship of the United States of
America to Aleksandr Solzhenitsyn, as specified in Bill SJR 36,
now before the House of Representatives.

                    Sincerely yours _____ (signature)

                                    _____ (address)

Honorable Joshua Eilberg, Chairman,

Subcommittee on Immigration, Citizenship and
International Law,
House of Representatives,
Washington, D. C. 20515

    Dear Mr. Eilberg:

    I respectfully request that your Subcommittee acts on Bill
SJR 36, authorizing the President to declare by proclamation that
Aleksandr I. Solzhenitsyn be an honorary citizen of the United
States of America.

               Sincerely yours _____(signature)

                               _____ (address)

BIBLIOGRAPHY

BIBLIOGRAPHY

PRIMARY SOURCES

Chichnikov, Zakhar. <u>Adventures in California of Zakhar Tchitchnikoff</u>,
    <u>1818-1828</u>. Los Angeles: Glen Dawson, 1956. Sheds light on
    the Russian colony of Fort Ross, California. The events des-
    cribed in the book were related by its author in 1878, partly
    from notes, and partly from memory.

Coxe, William. <u>Account of the Russian Discoveries Between Asia and</u>
    <u>America</u>. London, 1780. Furnishes interesting details related
    to the beginnings of Russian colonization in America, and its
    extension during the 18th century.

United States War Department. <u>The War of the Rebellion: A Compi-</u>
    <u>lation of the Official Records of the Union and Confederate</u>
    <u>Armies</u>. Washington, D. C.: G.P.O., 1880-1902. A multi
    volume set with several pages reflecting General John B. Tur-
    chin's activities, his reports to superiors, and opinions
    about him.

GENERAL BIBLIOGRAPHY

Andrews, Clarence L. <u>The Story of Alaska</u>. Caldwell, Idaho: The
    Caxton Printers, Ltd., 1938-1940. The first part of the book
    offers a very good coverage of the Russian period in Alaska,
    between 1728 and 1867. Splendid bibliographic information.

Brown, Francis and Roucek, Joseph. <u>One America: The History</u>,
    <u>Contributions and Present Problems of our Racial and National</u>
    <u>Minorities</u>. New York: Prentice-Hall, Inc., 1952. Short back-
    ground information on Russian Americans.

Eubank, Nancy. <u>The Russians in America</u>. Minneapolis, Minnesota:
    Learners Publications Company, 1973. A survey of Russian im-
    migration to the United States and Russian contributions to
    American life. Designed for teenagers.

Davis, Jerome. <u>The Russian Immigrant</u>. New York: The Mac Millan
    Company, 1922. Basic book on Russian Americans, with interest-
    ing data regarding early Russian settlements, immigration, eco-
    nomic conditions, social and religious life, and adjustments
    to the new environment.

Hutchinson, E. P. <u>Immigrants and Their Children: 1850-1950</u>. New
    York: John Wiley & Sons, Inc., 1956. Brings to light impor-
    tant social and economic aspects of Russian immigration in
    connection with and comparison to other ethnic groups. Based
    on the official 1950 United States Census data.

SPECIAL BIBLIOGRAPHY

Art and Music

Cross, Milton and Ewen, David. Milton Cross' Encyclopedia of the
    Great Composers and Their Music. New York: Doubleday and
    Company, Inc., 1962. Very good chapters on the life and works
    of Sergei Rachmaninoff, Igor Stravinsky, and others.

Cooking

Nicolaieff, Nina et al. The Art of Russian Cooking. Garden City,
    New Jersey: 1969. Flavorful recipes for Russian popular
    dishes.

Immigrant Experiences and Life

Argus, M. K. Moskow-On-The-Hudson. New York: Harper & Brothers,
    1951. The author describes his experiences as an immigrant
    who came from Russia in 1919 and settled in New York City.

Nabokov, Vladimir. Pnin. New York: Doubleday, 1957. A satiric
    novel depicting the life and character of an emigre Russian
    professor, a teacher in an upstate New York college.

Folk Songs and Dances

Bergman, Marion. The Russian-American Song and Dance Book. New
    York: A. S. Barnes & Company, 1947. Basic information on
    Russian folk songs, folk and national dances.

Organizations

Fisk, Margaret et al., ed. Encyclopedia of Associations. Detroit,
    Michigan: Gale Research Company, 1975. Lists Russian Ameri-
    can organizations and their specific activities.

Periodicals

Wynar, Lubomir. Encyclopedic Directory of Ethnic Newspapers and
    Periodicals in the United States. Littleton, Colorado: Li-
    braries Unlimited, Inc., 1972. Annotates all Russian Ameri-
    can periodicals and newspapers.

Radio Stations

American Council for Nationalities Service. Foreign Language Radio
    Stations in the U.S.A. New York: 1970. Lists all radio sta-
    tions broadcasting Russian language programs.

Religion

Jacquet, Constant H. Yearbook of American and Canadian Churches:
1974. Nashville, Tennessee: Abingdon Press, 1974. Furnishes
up to date statistical data on the denominations to which Russian Americans belong, as well as the way they are organized.

Mead, Frank S., ed. Handbook of Denominations in the United States.
Nashville, Tennessee: Abingdon Press, 1970. Describes the or-
ganizational structure of the Russian Orthodox and Catholic
churches.

Russian Language and Linguistics Study

Akhmanova, O. S., ed. Russian-English Dictionary. New York: 1966.
Good basic dictionary for students.

Folomkina, S., et al. The Learner's English-Russian Dictionary.
Cambridge, Massachusetts: The M.I.T. Press, 1963. An easy to
use basic vocabulary aid for the first years of Russian language
study, containing about 3,500 words.

Michailoff, Helen, et al. New Russian Self Taught. New York: Funk
& Wagnals, 1967. A basic guide providing an easy introduction
to reading, writing, speaking and understanding Russian.

Pei, Mario. The World Chief Languages. New York: S. F. Vanni,
1946. A noted linguist's views on the linguistic structure of
the Russian language, and its place in the family of Slavic
languages.

PERIODICAL LITERATURE

East, Ernest. "Lincoln's Russian General," Illinois State Historical
Journal, vol. 52 (Spring 1959).

McLaughlin, A. "Bright Side of Russian Immigration," Popular Science,
vol. 64 (November 1903).

Parry, Albert. "John Turchin: Russian General in the American
Civil War," The Russian Review, (April 1942).

"Teaching of Russian in the United States," School Life, vol. 40
(March 1958).

BIBLIOGRAPHY

Religion

APPENDICES

RUSSIAN AMERICAN INSTITUTIONS & ORGANIZATIONS

ALL-RUSSIAN MONARCHIST FRONT (ARMF)
    520 West 163rd Street
    New York, New York 10032

AMERICAN RUSSIAN AID ASSOCIATION
    349 West 86th Street
    New York, New York 10024

AMERICAN RUSSIAN SLAVONIC DEMOCRATIC CLUB
    1465 Fulton Avenue
    Bronx, New York 10456

AMERICAN SOCIETY FOR RUSSIAN NAVAL HISTORY
    349 West 86th Street
    New York, New York 10024

ASSOCIATION OF RUSSIAN IMPERIAL NAVAL OFFICERS IN AMERICA
    349 West 86th Street
    New York, New York 10024

FEDERATED RUSSIAN ORTHODOX CLUBS
    84 East Market Place
    Wilkes Barre, Pennsylvania 18701

FUND FOR THE RELIEF OF RUSSIAN WRITERS & SCIENTISTS IN EXILE
    243 West 56th Street
    New York, New York 10019

RUSSIAN AMERICAN CONGRESS
    222 West 108th Street
    New York, New York 10024

RUSSIAN BROTHERHOOD ORGANIZATION OF THE U.S.A.
    1733 Spring Garden Street
    Philadelphia, Pennsylvania 19130

RUSSIAN CHILDREN'S WELFARE SOCIETY
    59 East Second Street
    New York, New York 10003

RUSSIAN INDEPENDENT MUTUAL AID SOCIETY
    917 North Wood Street
    Chicago, Illinois 60622

RUSSIAN NOBILITY ASSOCIATION IN AMERICA
    971 First Avenue
    New York, New York 10022

RUSSIAN ORTHODOX CATHOLIC MUTUAL AID SOCIETY OF U.S.A.
    84 Market Street
    Wilkes Barre, Pennsylvania 18701

RUSSIAN ORTHODOX CATHOLIC WOMEN'S MUTUAL AID SOCIETY
    1230 Greentree Road
    Pittsburgh, Pennsylvania 15220

THE RUSSIAN ORTHODOX CHURCH IN THE U.S.A.
    St. Nicholas Patriarchal Cathedral
    15 East 97th Street
    New York, New York 10029

THE RUSSIAN ORTHODOX CHURCH OF AMERICA
    59 East Second Street
    New York, New York 10003

RUSSIAN ORTHODOX CHURCH OUTSIDE RUSSIA
    75 East 93rd Street
    New York, New York 10028

RUSSIAN ORTHODOX FRATERNITY LIUBOV
    402 Delaware Street
    Jermyn, Pennsylvania 18433

RUSSIAN PEOPLE'S CENTER
    545 West 142nd Street
    New York, New York 10031

RUSSIAN STUDENT FUND
    845 Third Avenue
    New York, New York 10031

SOCIETY OF THE RUSSIAN VETERANS OF THE WORLD WARS
    2041 Lyon Street
    San Francisco, California 94115

TOLSTOY FOUNDATION
    250 West 57th Street
    New York, New York 10019

UNITED RUSSIAN BROTHERHOOD OF AMERICA
    333 Boulevard of the Allies
    Pittsburgh, Pennsylvania 15222

RUSSIAN AMERICAN PERIODICALS

NOVAYA ZARYA
    2078 Sutter Street
    San Francisco, California 94115

NOVOYE RUSSKOYE SLOVO
    243 West 56th Street
    New York, New York 10019

NOVYJ ZHURNAL
    The New Review, Inc.
    2700 Broadway
    New York, New York 10019

THE ORTHODOX HERALD
    116 Eastridge Drive
    San Antonio, Texas 78227

PRAVOSLAVNAYA ZHIZN
    Holy Trinity Monastery
    Jordanville, New York 13361

ROSSIYA
    216 West 18th Street
    New York, New York 10011

THE RUSSIAN REVIEW
    The Hoover Institution
    Stanford, California 94305

RUSSKAYA ZHIZN
    2458 Sutter Street
    San Francisco, California 94115

RUSSKO AMERICANSKY PRAVOSLAVNY VESTNIK
    Russian American Orthodox Messenger
    59 East Second Street
    New York, New York 10003

ST. VLADIMIR'S THEOLOGICAL QUARTERLY
    575 Scarsdale Road
    Crestwood, New York 10707

TOLSTOY FOUNDATION NEWSLETTER
    250 West 57th Street
    New York, New York 10019

ZNAMYA ROSSII
    3544 Broadway
    New York, New York 10031

RUSSIAN IN AMERICAN COLLEGES & UNIVERSITIES

The following is a list of American colleges and universities offering courses in Russian studies.

ALABAMA
    University of Alabama
    University of South Alabama

ALASKA
    Alaska Methodist University
    University of Alaska

ARIZONA
    Arizona State University
    Northern Arizona University
    University of Arizona

CALIFORNIA
    California State University
    Monterey Institute of Foreign
            Studies
    Occidental College
    Stanford University
    University of California
    University of San Francisco
    University of Southern Cali-
            fornia

COLORADO
    Colorado Women's College
    Southern Colorado State
            College
    University of Denver

CONNECTICUT
    Connecticut College
    Southern Connecticut State
            University
    Trinity College
    University of Connecticut
    Wesleyan University
    Yale University

DELEWARE
    University of Deleware
    American University
    Gallaudet College
    George Washington University
    Georgetown University
    Howard University
    Trinity College

FLORIDA
    Eckerd College
    Florida International
            University
    Florida State University
    New College
    Stetson University
    University of Florida
    University of Miami
    University of South Florida

GEORGIA
    Emory University
    Morehouse College

HAWAII
    University of Hawaii

ILLINOIS
    Illinois State University
    Knox College
    Northern Illinois University
    Northwestern University
    Roosevelt University
    University of Chicago
    University of Illinois
    Western Illinois University

INDIANA
    Ball State University
    De Pauw University
    Indiana State University
    Purdue University
    University of Notre Dame

IOWA
    Cornell College
    Iowa State University
    University of Iowa

KANSAS
    University of Kansas

KENTUCKY
    Eastern Kentucky University
    University of Kentucky
    Western Kentucky University

LOUISIANA
  Louisiana State University
  Loyola University
  Tulane University

MAINE
  Bowdoin College

MARYLAND
  University of Maryland

MASSACHUSETTS
  Amherst College
  Boston University
  Brandeis University
  Clark University
  College of Holy Cross
  Harvard University
  Radcliffe College
  Smith College
  Tufts University
  University of Massachusetts
  Wellesley College
  Wheaton College
  Williams College

MICHIGAN
  Central Michigan University
  Michigan State University
  Oakland University
  University of Michigan
  Wayne State University
  Western Michigan University

MINNESOTA
  Bemidji State College
  College of St. Catherine
  College of St. Teresa
  College of St. Thomas
  Hamline University
  Mankato State College
  St. Mary's College
  St. Olaf College
  University of Minnesota

MISSISSIPPI
  University of Mississippi
  University of Southern Mis-
          sissippi

MISSOURI
  St. Louis University
  University of Missouri

Westminster College

MONTANA
  University of Montana

NEBRASKA
  University of Nebraska

NEW HAMPSHIRE
  Dartmouth College

NEW JERSEY
  Fairleigh Dickinson University
  Rider College
  Rutgers State University

NEW MEXICO
  New Mexico State University

NEW YORK
  Alfred University
  Barnard College
  Brooklyn College
  City College
  Colgate University
  Columbia University
  Cornell University
  Fordham University
  Hartwick College
  Hofstra University
  Hunter College
  Manhattanville College
  New York University
  Queens College
  State University of New York
  Syracuse University
  Union College
  University of Rochester
  Vassar College

NORTH CAROLINA
  Duke University
  East Carolina University
  Queens College
  University of North Carolina

OHIO
  Antioch College
  Bowling Green State University
  Case Western Reserve University
  Cleveland State University
  College of Wooster
  Denison University

Hiram College
Kent State University
Miami University
Oberlin College
Ohio State University
Ohio University
University of Akron
University of Cincinnati
Wright State University
Youngstown State University

OKLAHOMA
Oklahoma City University
University of Oklahoma
University of Tulsa

OREGON
Oregon State University
Portland State University
Reed College
University of Oregon
Willamette University

PENNSYLVANIA
Allegheny College
Alliance College
Bryn Mawr College
Bucknell University
California State College
Carnegie-Mellon University
Clarion State College
Dickinson College
Edinboro State College
Franklin & Marshall College
Haverford College
Indiana University
Kutztown State College
Lafayette College
La Salle College
Lycoming College
Millersville State College
Muhlenberg College
Penn State University
Swarthmore College
Temple University
University of Pennsylvania
University of Pittsburgh
West Chester State College

RHODE ISLAND
Brown University

TENNESSEE
University of South Tennessee
University of Tennessee
Vanderbilt University

TEXAS
Baylor University
Rice University
University of Texas

UTAH
Brigham Young University
University of Utah

VERMONT
Bennington College
Middlebury College
Norwich University
University of Vermont

VIRGINIA
Madison College
Mary Washington College
Old Dominion University
Randolph-Macon Woman's
        College
University of Richmond
University of Virginia

WASHINGTON
Eastern Washington State
        College
University of Washington
Western Washington State
        College

WEST VIRGINIA
West Virginia University

WISCONSIN
Lawrence University
Ripon College
University of Wisconsin

WYOMING
University of Wyoming

THE RUSSIAN ALPHABET AND ITS ENGLISH PRONUNCIATION

А а - like Art	С с - like Sort
Б б - like Book	Т т - like Train
В в - like Visit	У у - like mOOn
Г г - like Go	Ф ф - like Fog
Д д - like Dog	Х х - like KHaki
Е е - like YEllow	Ц ц - like caTS
Ё ё - like YOUrs	Ч ч - like lunCH
Ж ж - like pleaSure	Ш ш - like SHare
З з - like Zero	Щ щ - like miSCHief
И и - like machIne	Ъ ъ - indicates nonpalatization of a preceeding consonant
Й й - like boY	Ы ы - like mIster
К к - like Kelp	ь ь - indicates palatization of a preceeding consonant
Л л - like Lemon	Э э - like Ebony
М м - like Motor	Ю ю - like YUle
Н н - like Noon	Я я - like YAk
О о - like Ox	
П п - like Pen	
Р р - like Red	

RUSSIAN PROVERBS

He who speaks, sows; who listens reaps.

Don't praise marriage on the third day, but after the third year.

A strange illusion is to suppose that beauty is goodness.

He who fears a sparrow will never sow millet.

Time does not bow to you; you must bow to time.

Fear the goat from the front, the horse from the rear, and man from all sides.

RUSSIAN LANGUAGE DECLARED AS MOTHER TONGUE BY
NATIVITY, PARENTAGE AND RACE

YEARS	TOTAL	NATIVES OF NATIVE, FOREIGN BORN, OR MIXED PARENTAGE	FOREIGN BORN
1910	95,137	37,211	57,926
1940	571,100	214,160	356,940
1970	334,615	185,338	149,277

UNITED STATES CENSUS - 1970

		WHITE	OTHER RACES
TOTAL	334,615	332,881	1,313
TOTAL NATIVE OF NATIVE PARENTAGE	30,665	29,962	554
NATIVE OF FOREIGN OR MIXED PARENTAGE	154,673	154,275	307
FOREIGN BORN	149,277	148,644	452

Source: U. S. Department of Commerce. 1970 Census of Population: Detailed Characteristics - U.S. Summary. Washington, D. C.: U. S. Government Printing Office, 1973.

NAME INDEX